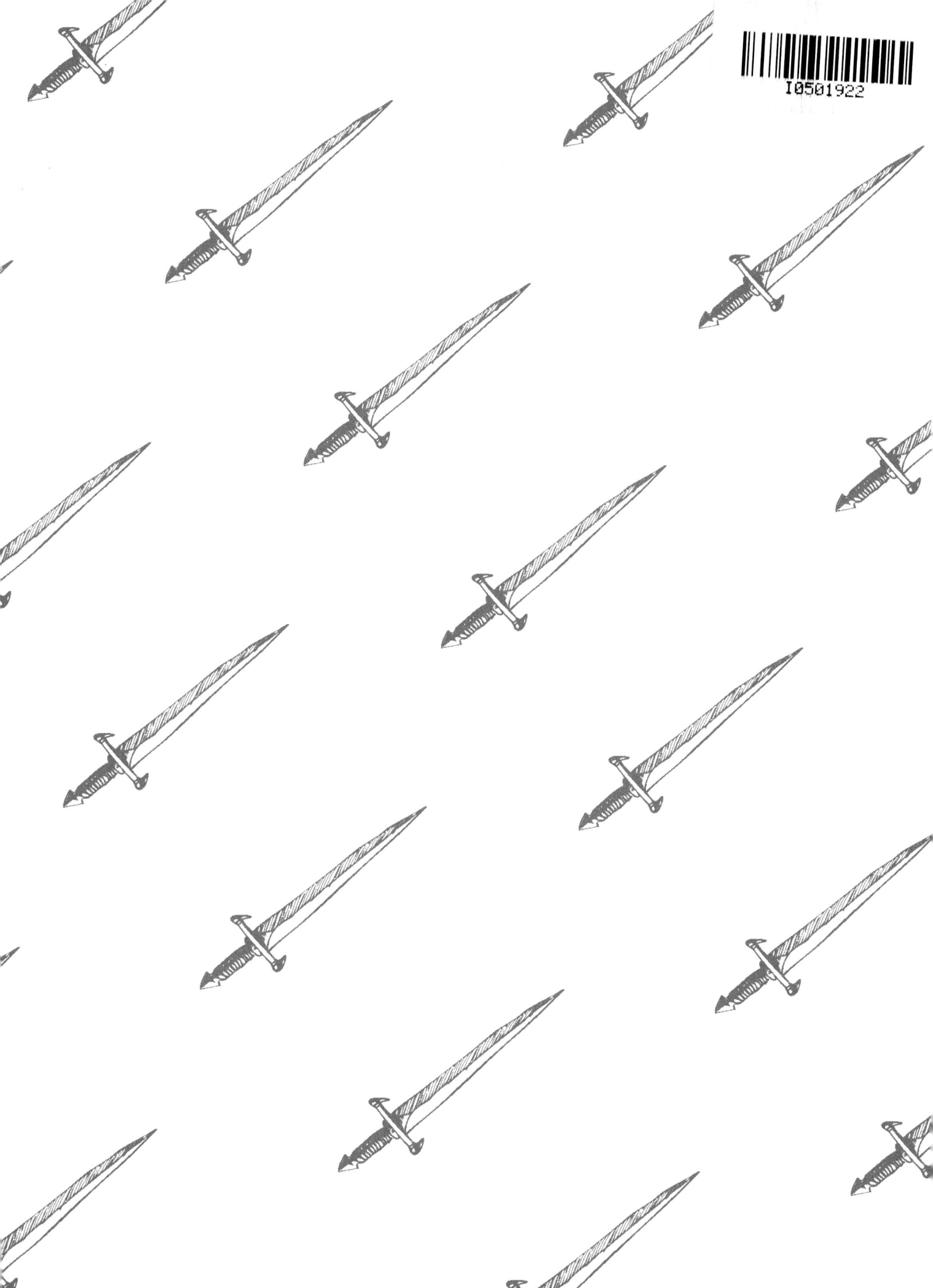

Tales of Gwyn

Copyright © 2024 / Twilight Citadel

All the words and pictures in this picture book, "Tales of Gwyn," belong only to

Matthew Smith. This means nobody else can copy or share them without

the owner's permission. If you want to use anything from this book, you need

to ask their permission first. You can't just copy it.

For permission requests, please contact the owner at:

twilightcitadel1@gmail.com

All rights reserved.

Published by Amazon KDP at Seattle, Washington, United States.

ISBN: 9798320848426

Tales of Gwyn

Created by
Matt Smith

humans

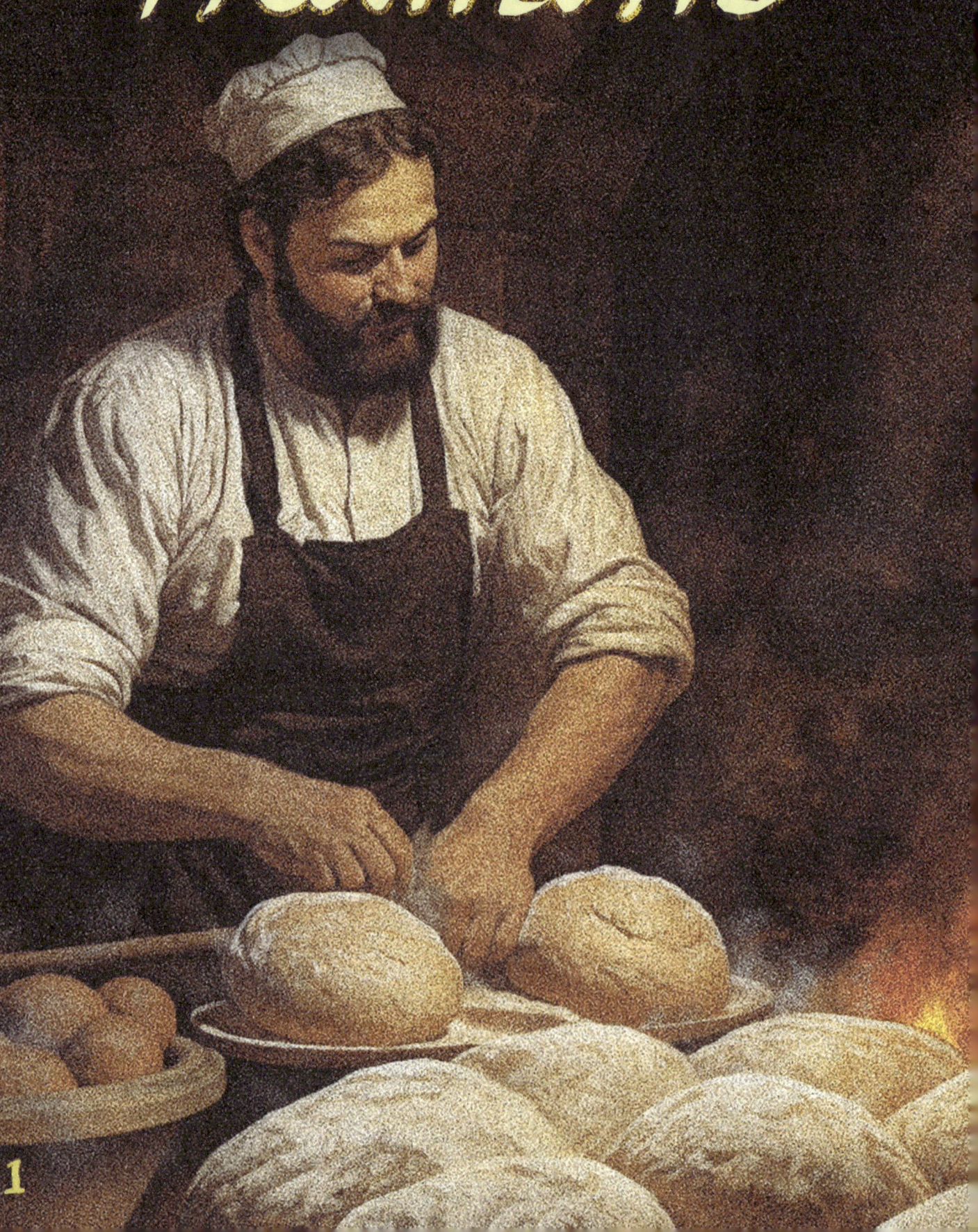

1

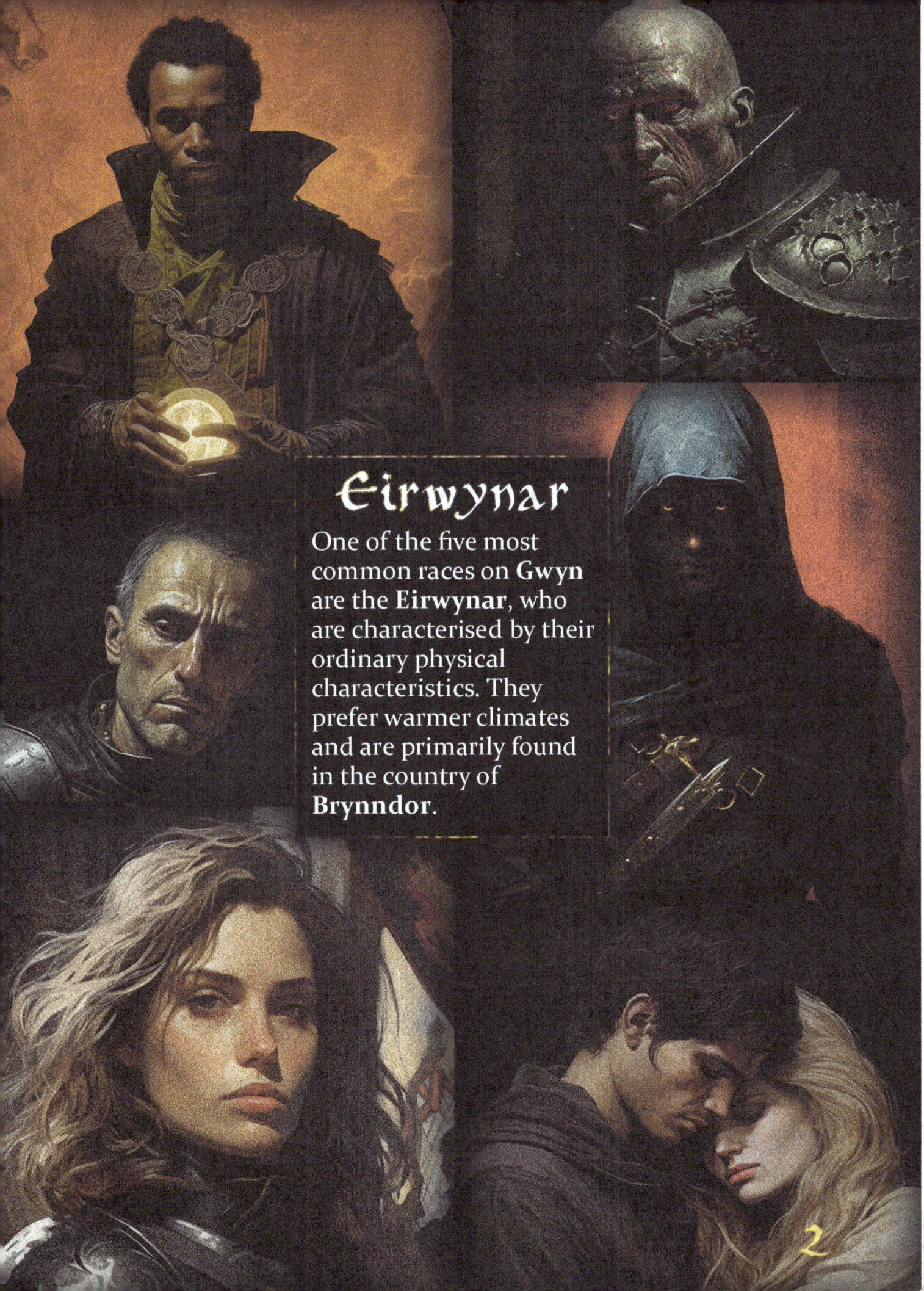

Eirwynar

One of the five most common races on **Gwyn** are the **Eirwynar**, who are characterised by their ordinary physical characteristics. They prefer warmer climates and are primarily found in the country of **Brynndor**.

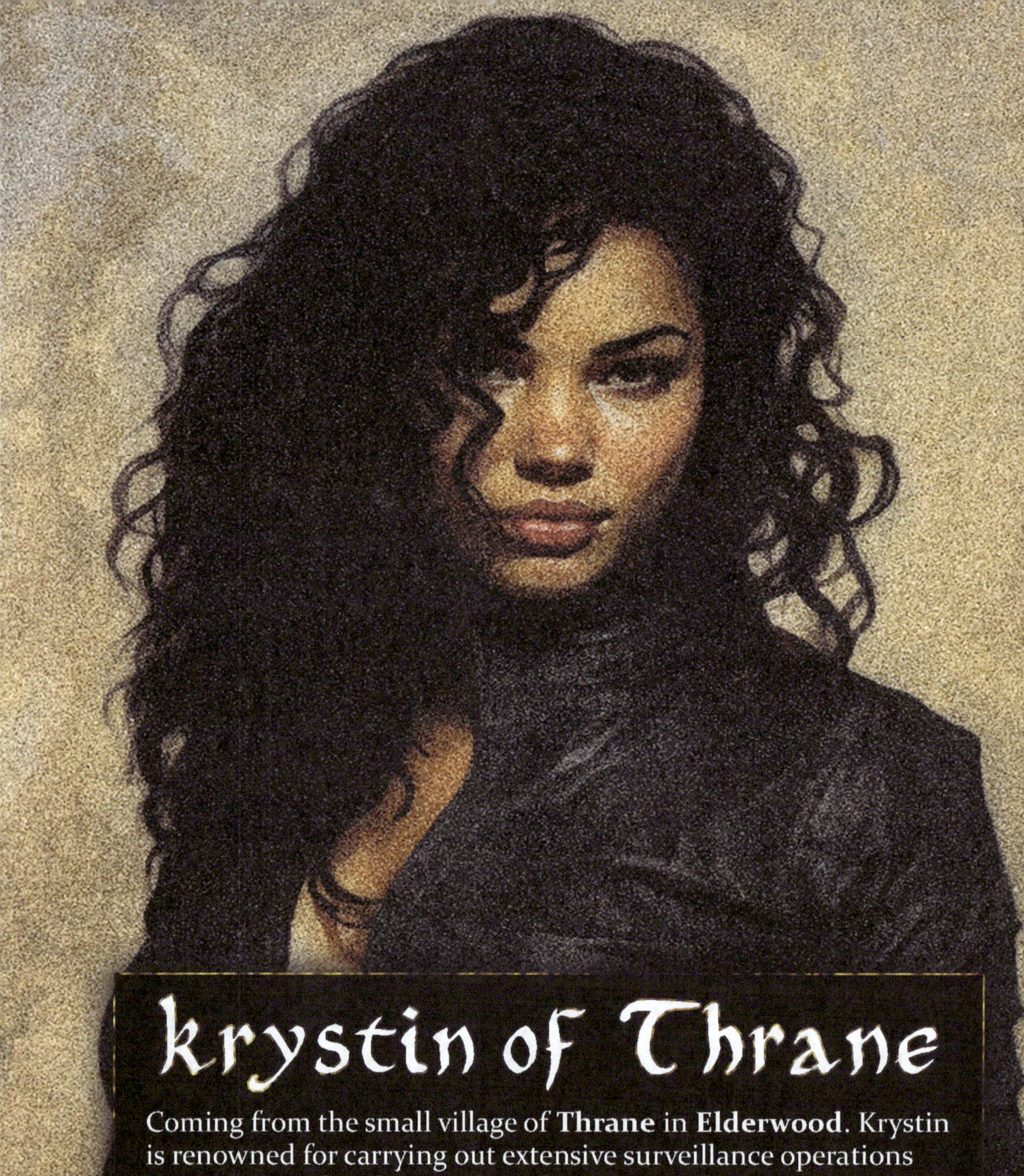

krystin of Thrane

Coming from the small village of **Thrane** in **Elderwood**. Krystin is renowned for carrying out extensive surveillance operations across **Brynndor** that result in the capture of prominent cult leaders and usurpers endangering the principles of the **Arcane Sovereign Guild**. She was sent to grow up in a covert camp that specialises in teaching skilled mercenaries and thieves.

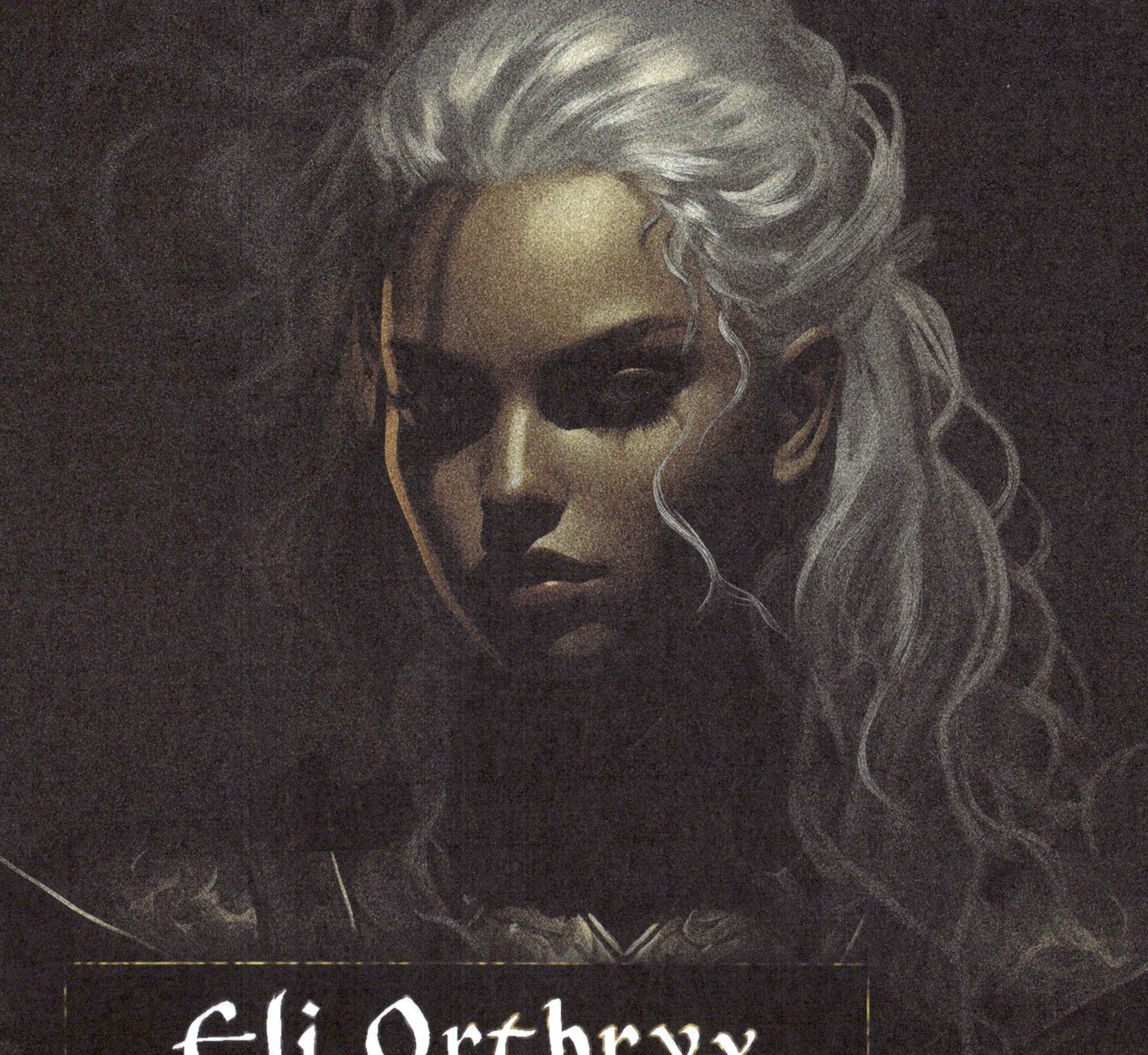

Eli Orthryx

Eli originates from **Thundersgate**, the only major city in the **Stormspear** region. She's the oldest daughter of the **Orthryx** family, a respected noble lineage. With a vast military experience, she gained the title of General in the northern battalions of **Brynndor**. Her mind for strategy and her tendency towards cruelty became widely recognised. Eli is highly skilled in lightning magic and fights with a short sword and dagger simultaneously.

Wizards

The world of **Gwyn** is home to wizards, whose abilities can only be attained by rigorous training, elemental mastery, and harnessing the lingering essence of the gods left after **The God Wars**.

There are many areas of spell mastery, such as; nature elements, summoning, curses and hexes, enchanting, necromancy, astral alteration, alchemy, and illusions. Typically, wizards specialise in one of these areas. Over the course of their lives, exceptionally talented wizards become proficient in multiple of these abilities.

All creatures in **Gwyn** are born with the ability to hone their connection to the essence of gods, the degree of soul purity in each creature determines which kind of magic they are pre-disposed to.

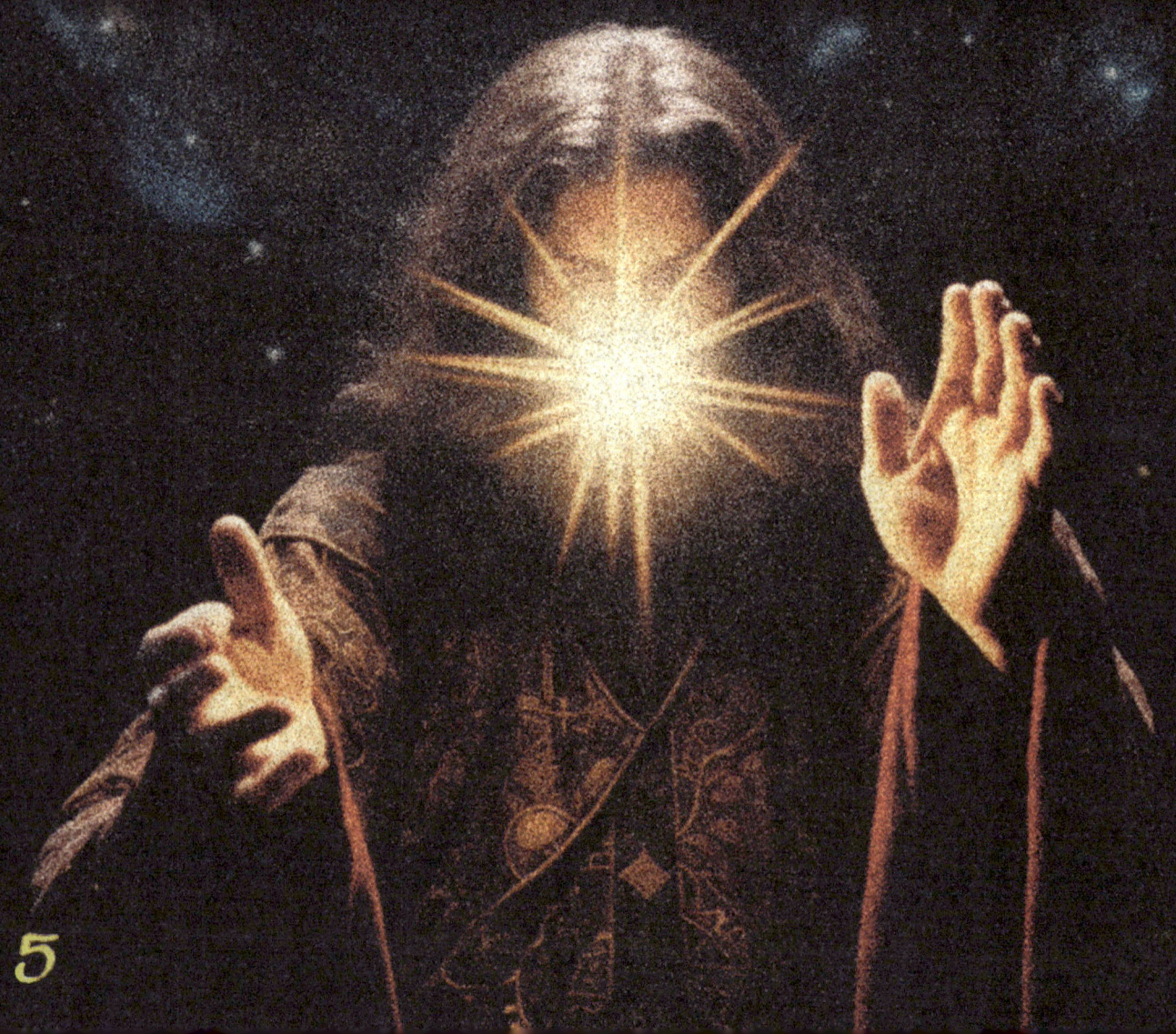

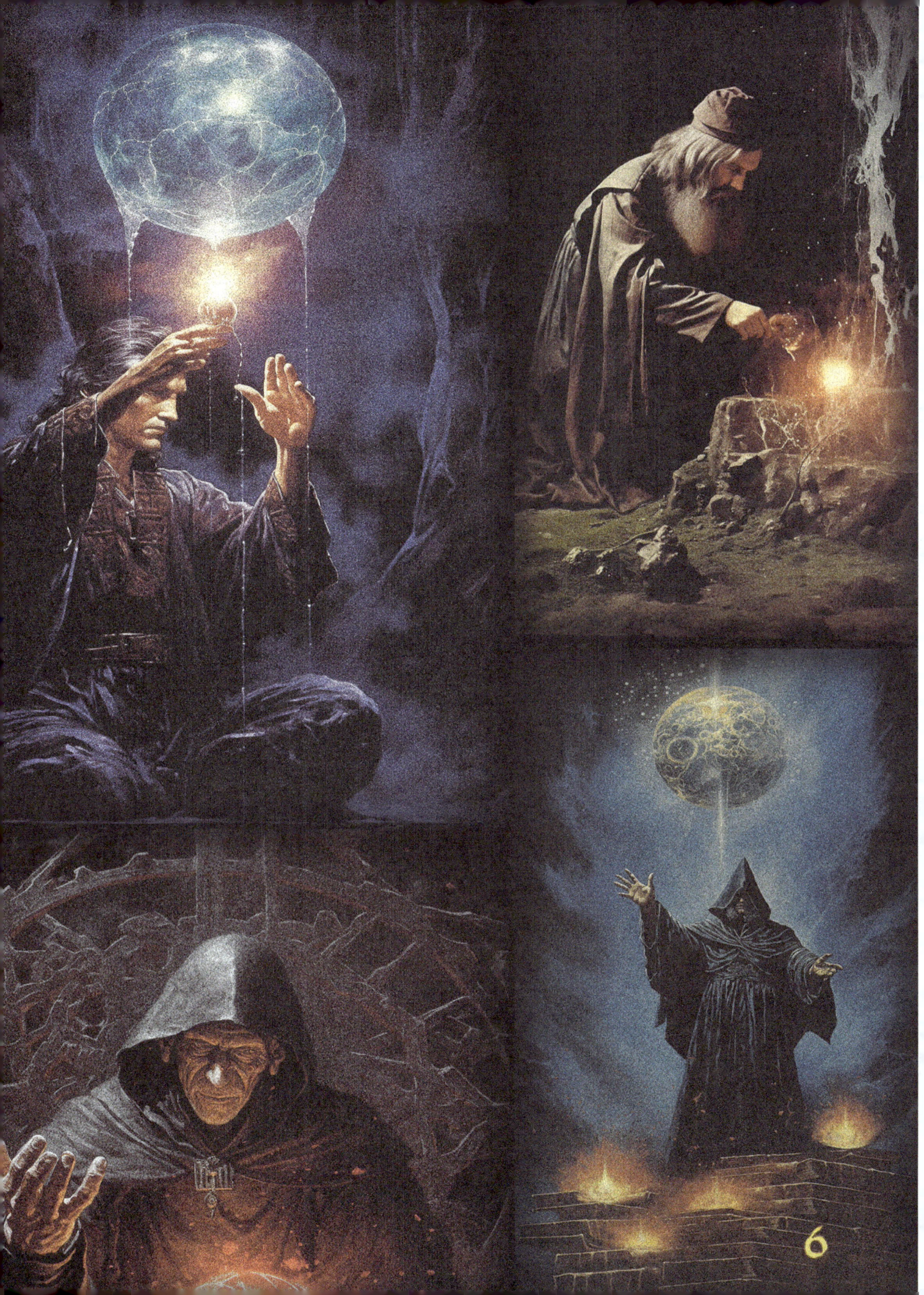

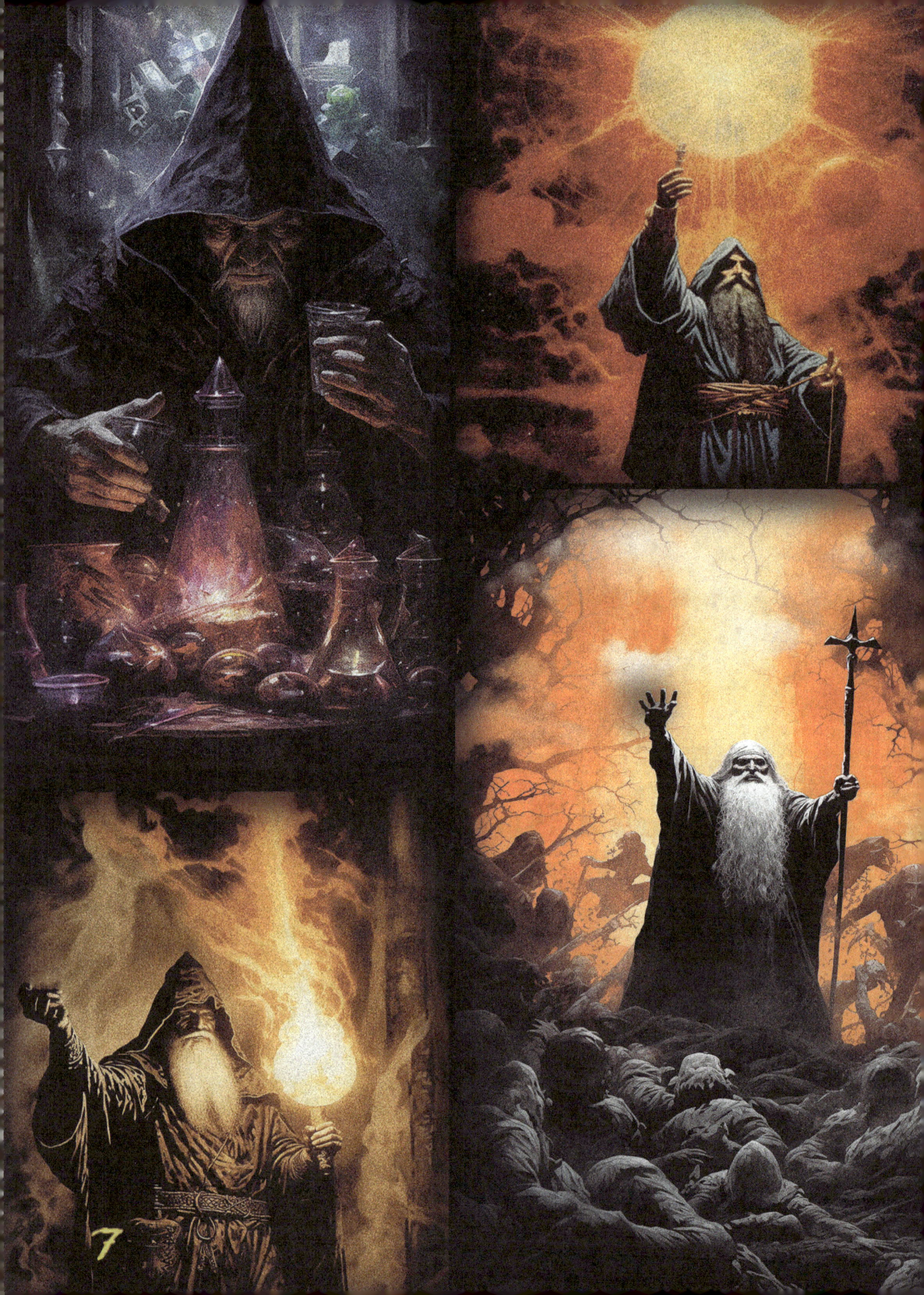

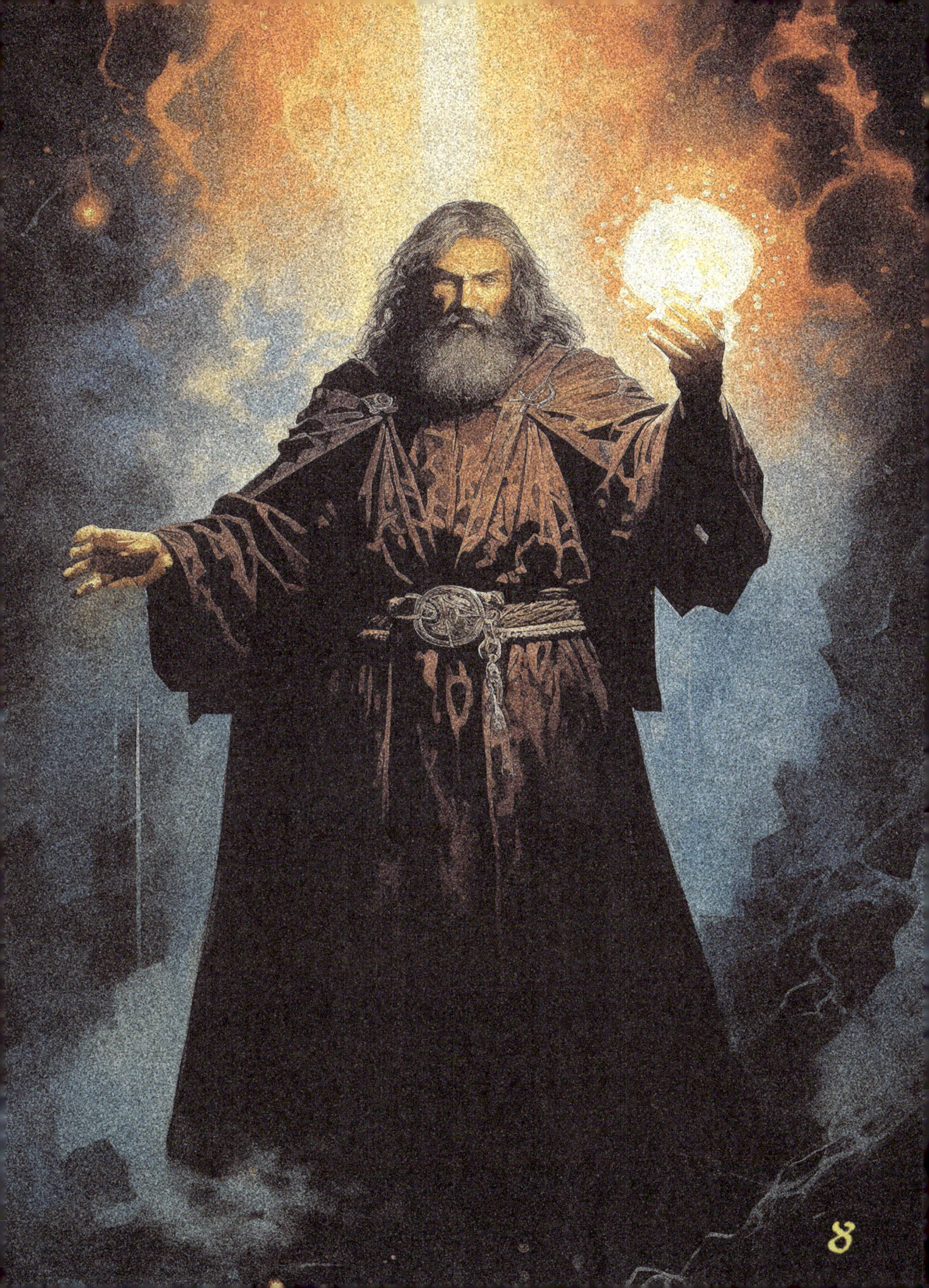

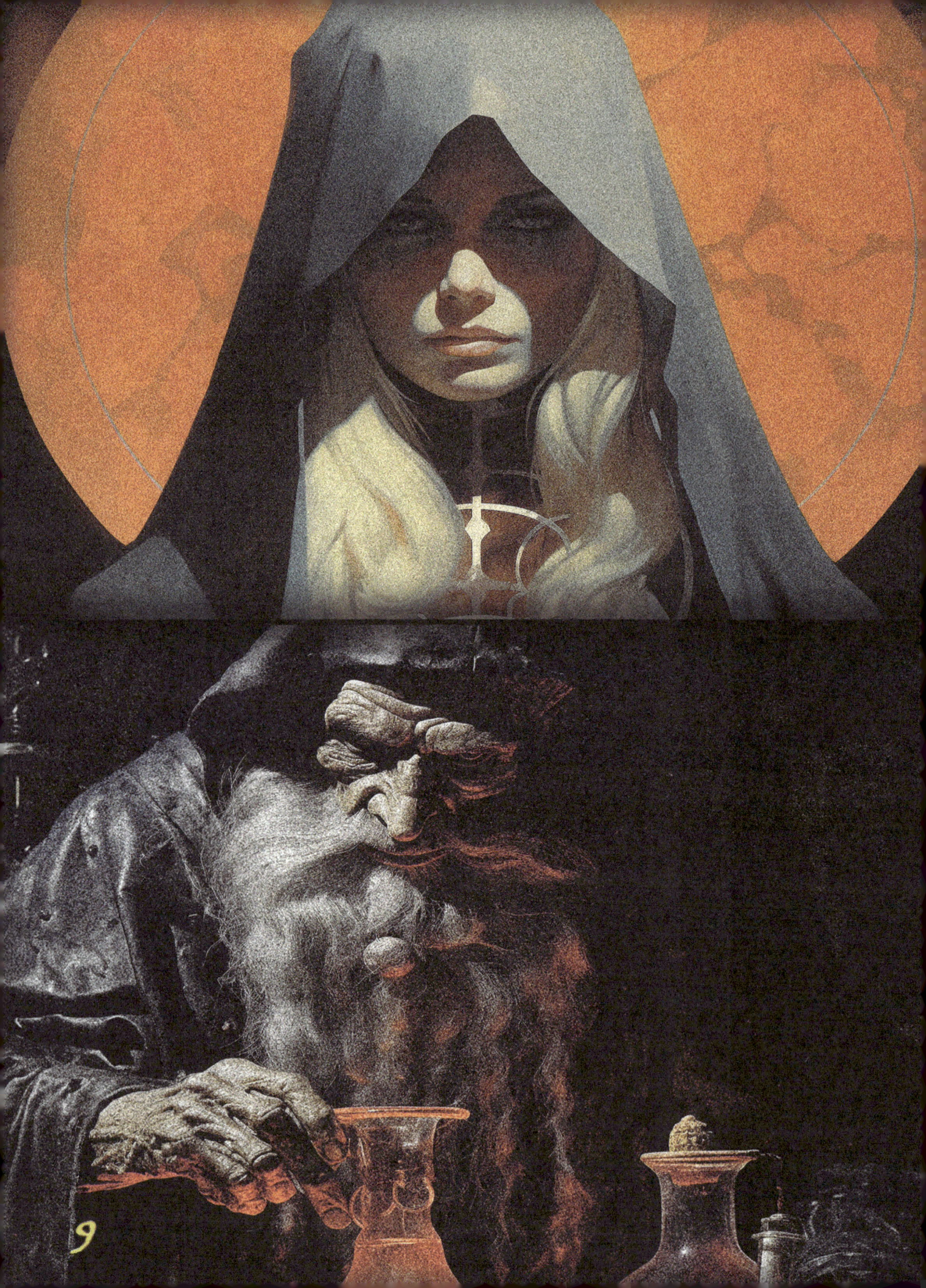

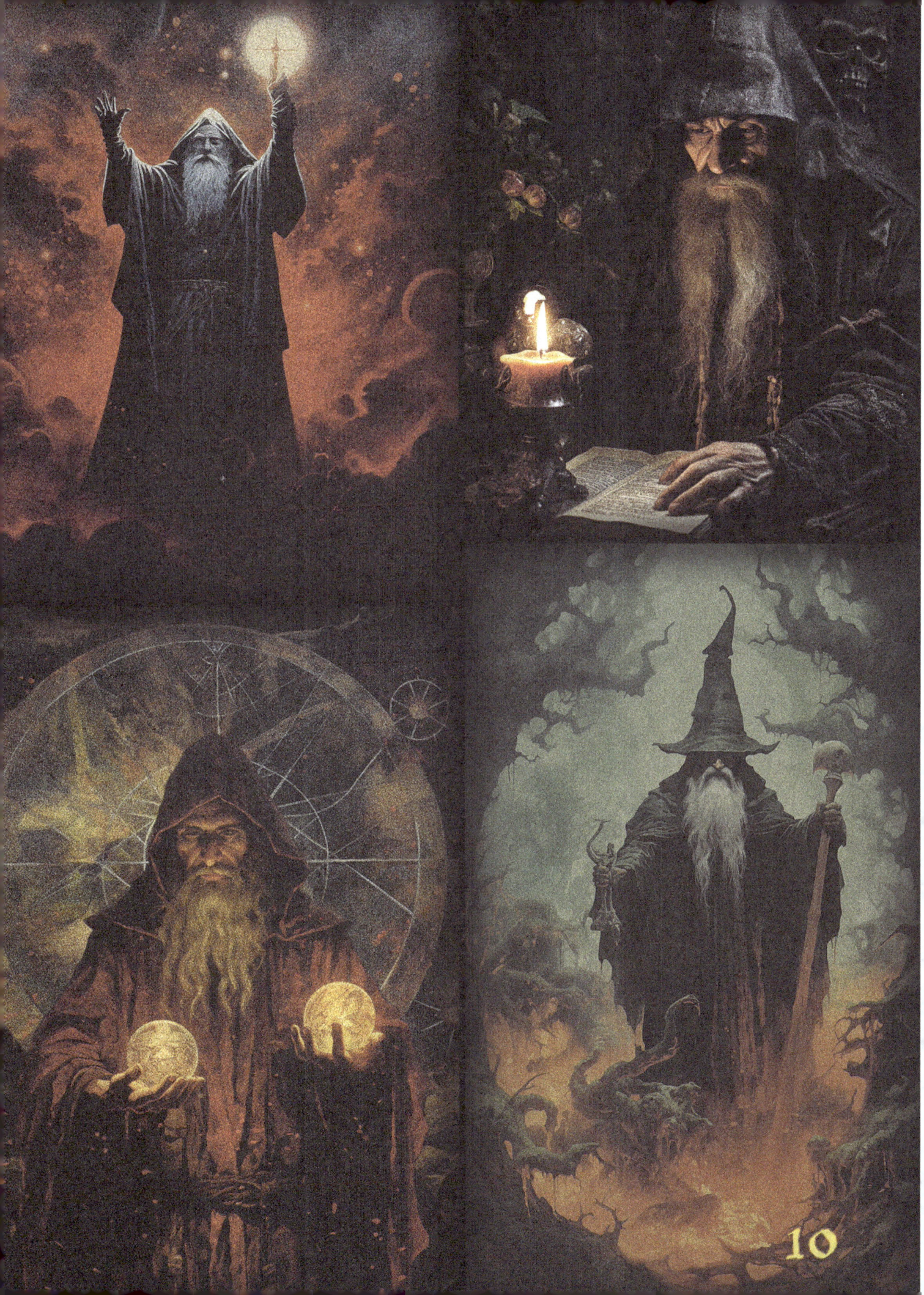

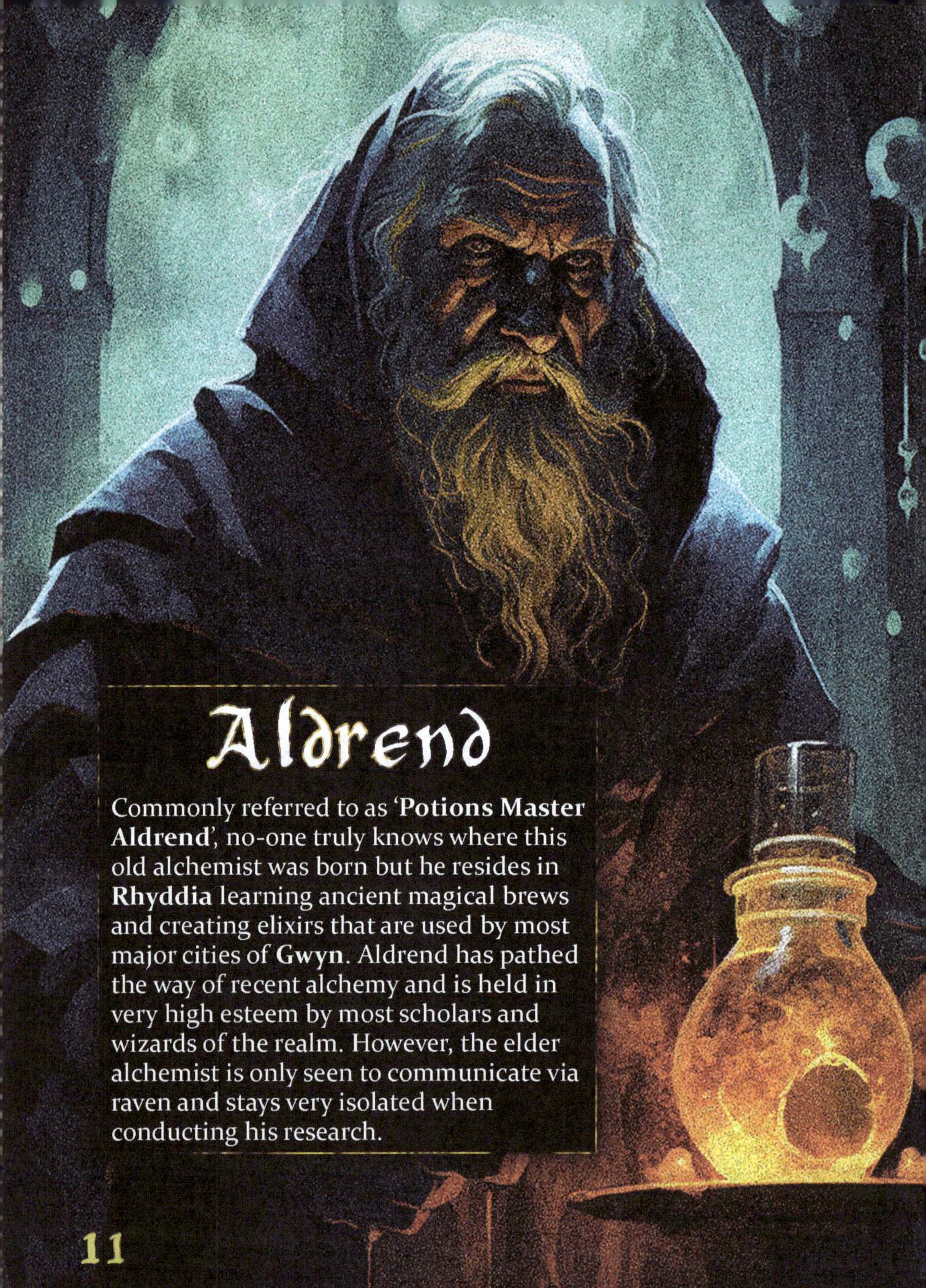

Aldrend

Commonly referred to as '**Potions Master Aldrend**', no-one truly knows where this old alchemist was born but he resides in **Rhyddia** learning ancient magical brews and creating elixirs that are used by most major cities of **Gwyn**. Aldrend has pathed the way of recent alchemy and is held in very high esteem by most scholars and wizards of the realm. However, the elder alchemist is only seen to communicate via raven and stays very isolated when conducting his research.

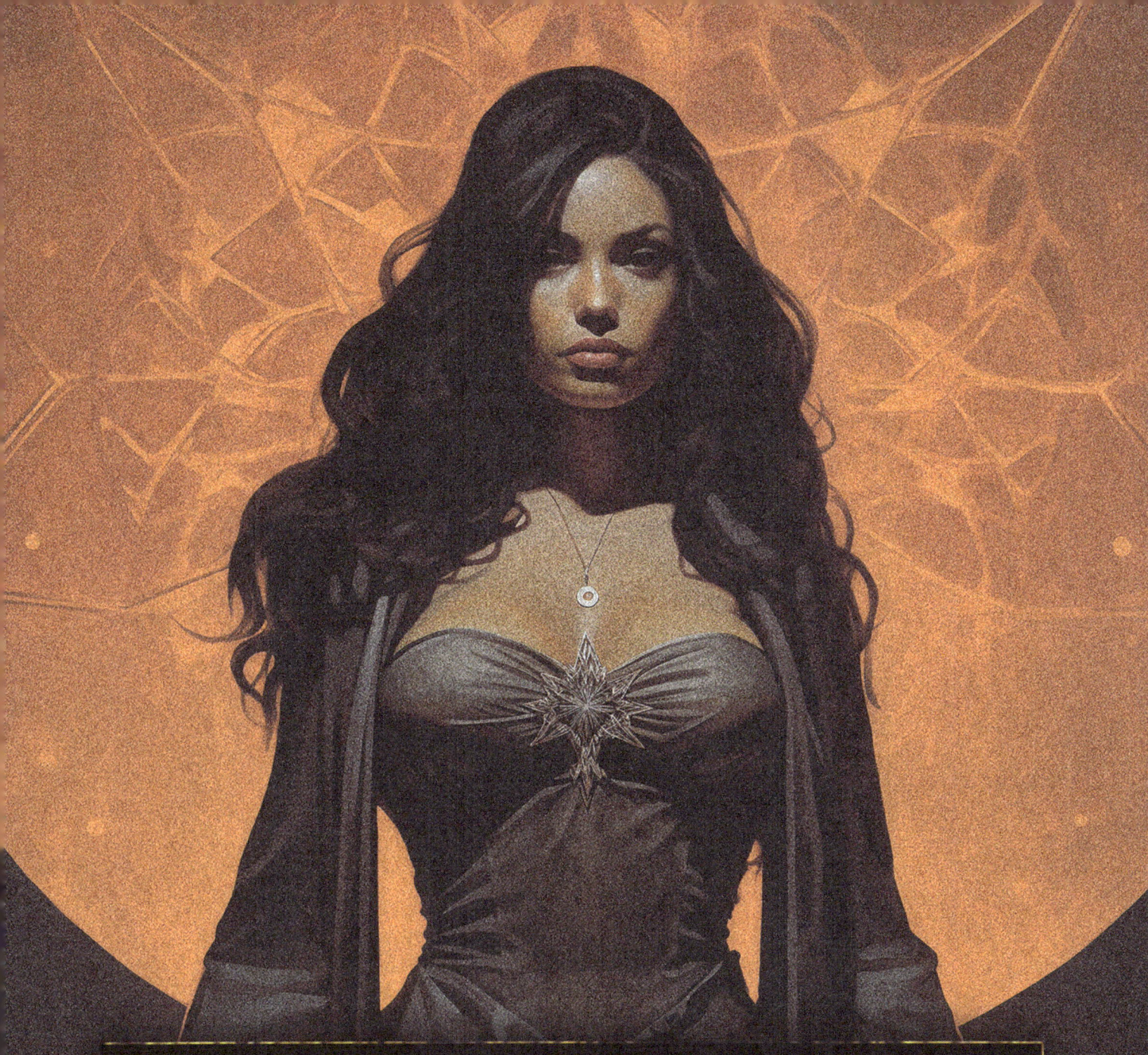

Lina the Sorceress

Lina is from the ocean-side town of **Willow**, one of many aligning the southern coast of **Ebonholt**. This sorceress has honed her abilities in conjuration, enchanting and mastery of earth magic. Gaining proficient skill in three magic disciplines has given her a formidable reputation in the southern region of **Tanbryn**. She is known to introduce young women into magic and they are always bewildered by her abilities, amassing many students.

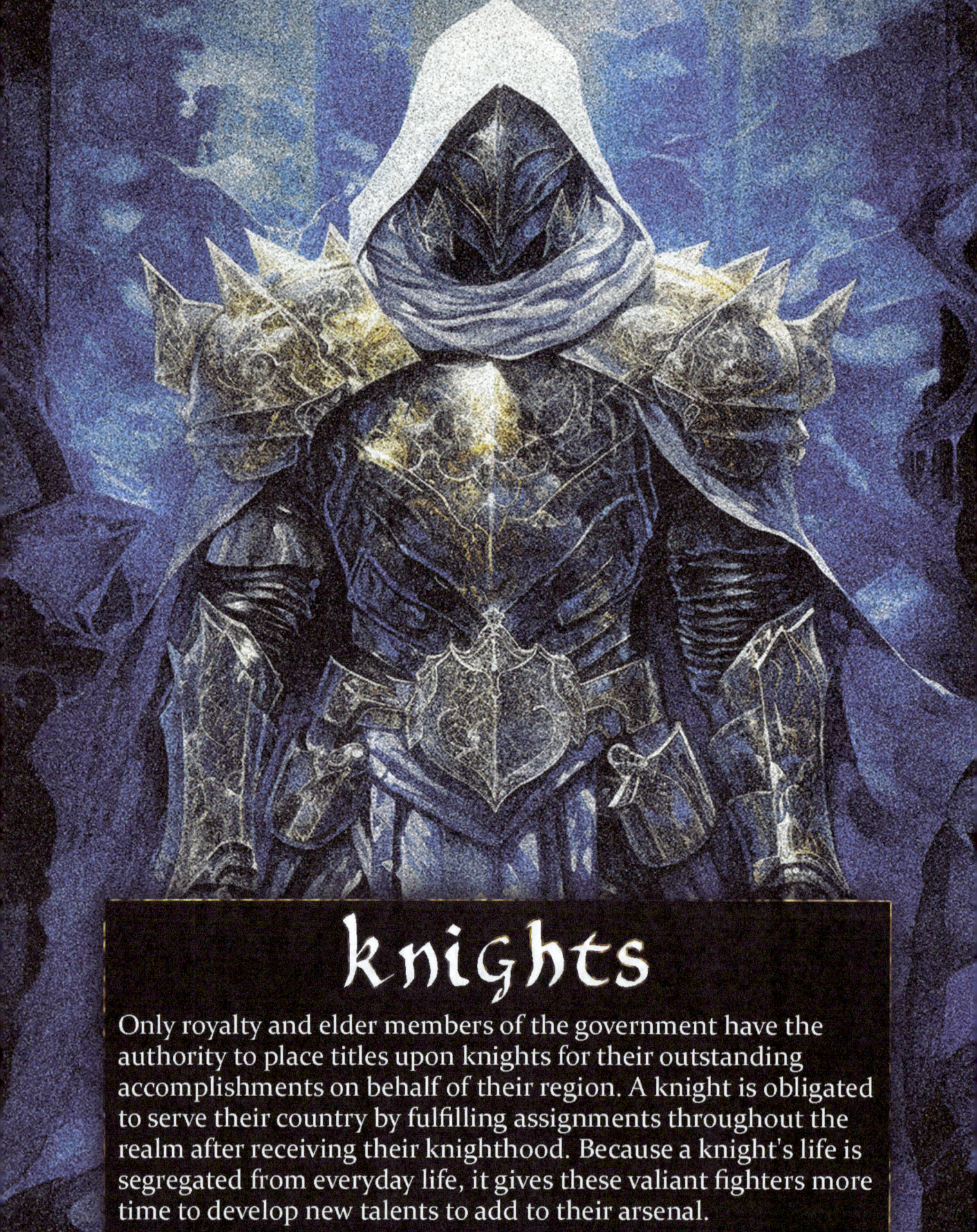

knights

Only royalty and elder members of the government have the authority to place titles upon knights for their outstanding accomplishments on behalf of their region. A knight is obligated to serve their country by fulfilling assignments throughout the realm after receiving their knighthood. Because a knight's life is segregated from everyday life, it gives these valiant fighters more time to develop new talents to add to their arsenal.

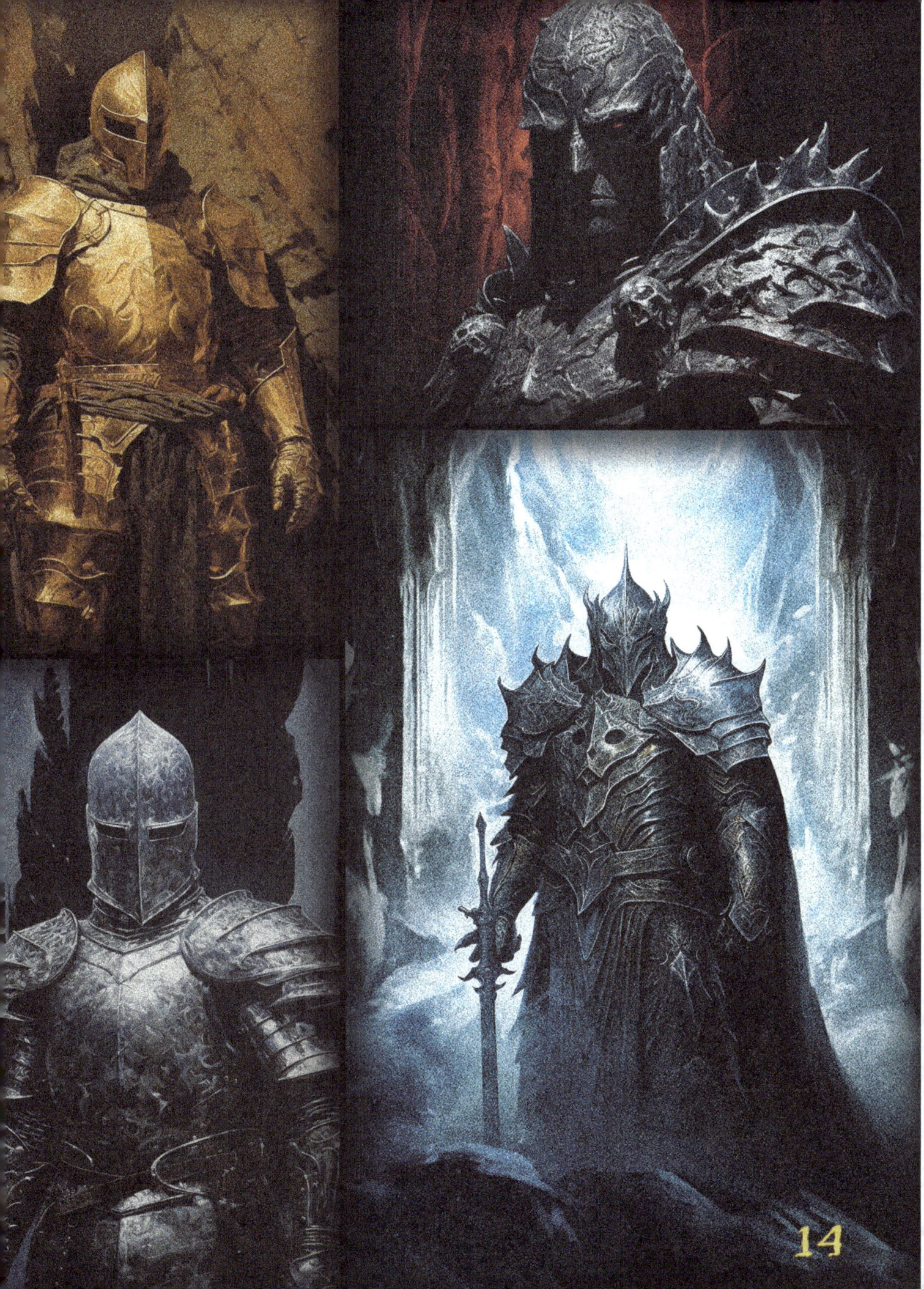

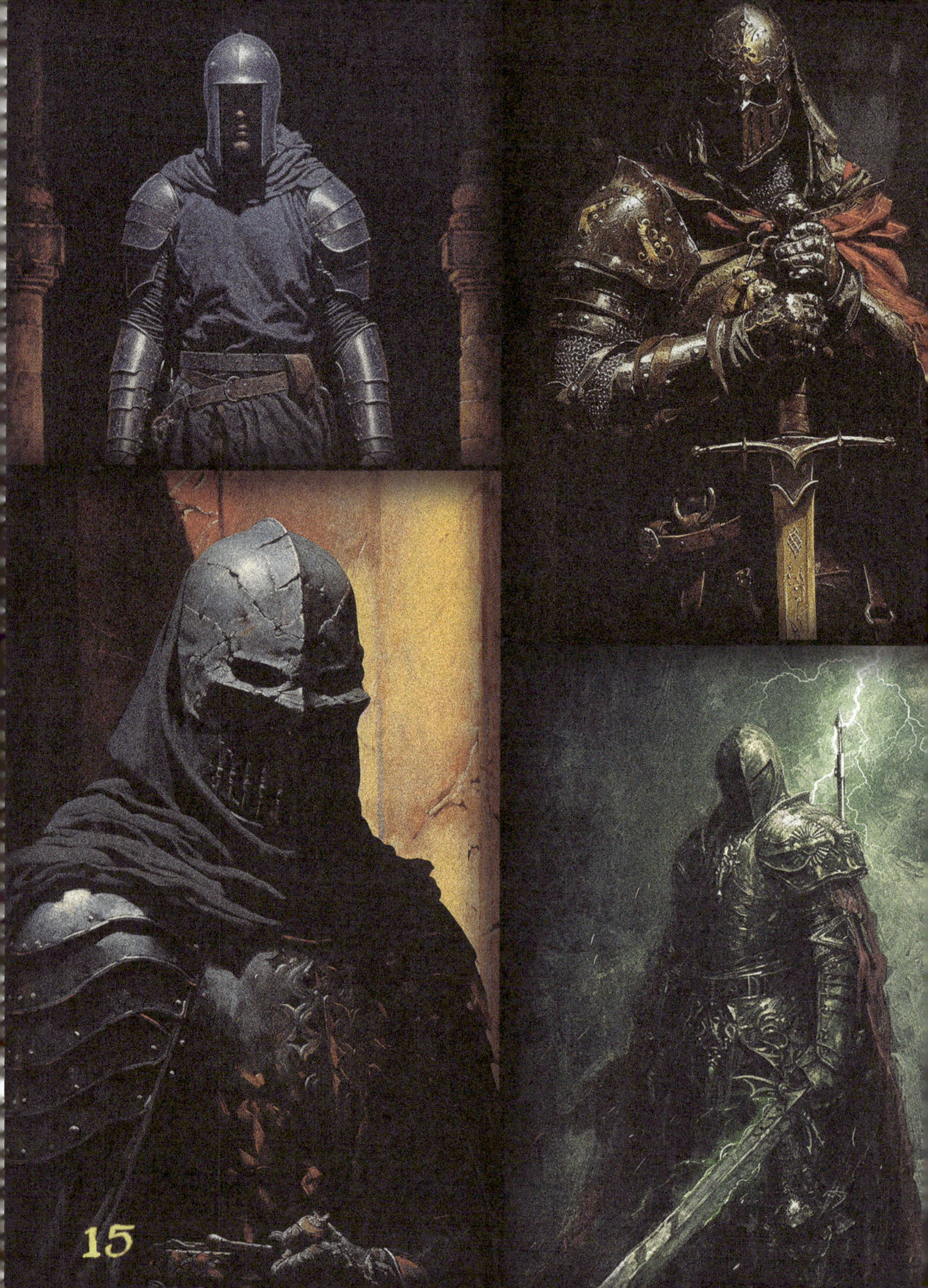

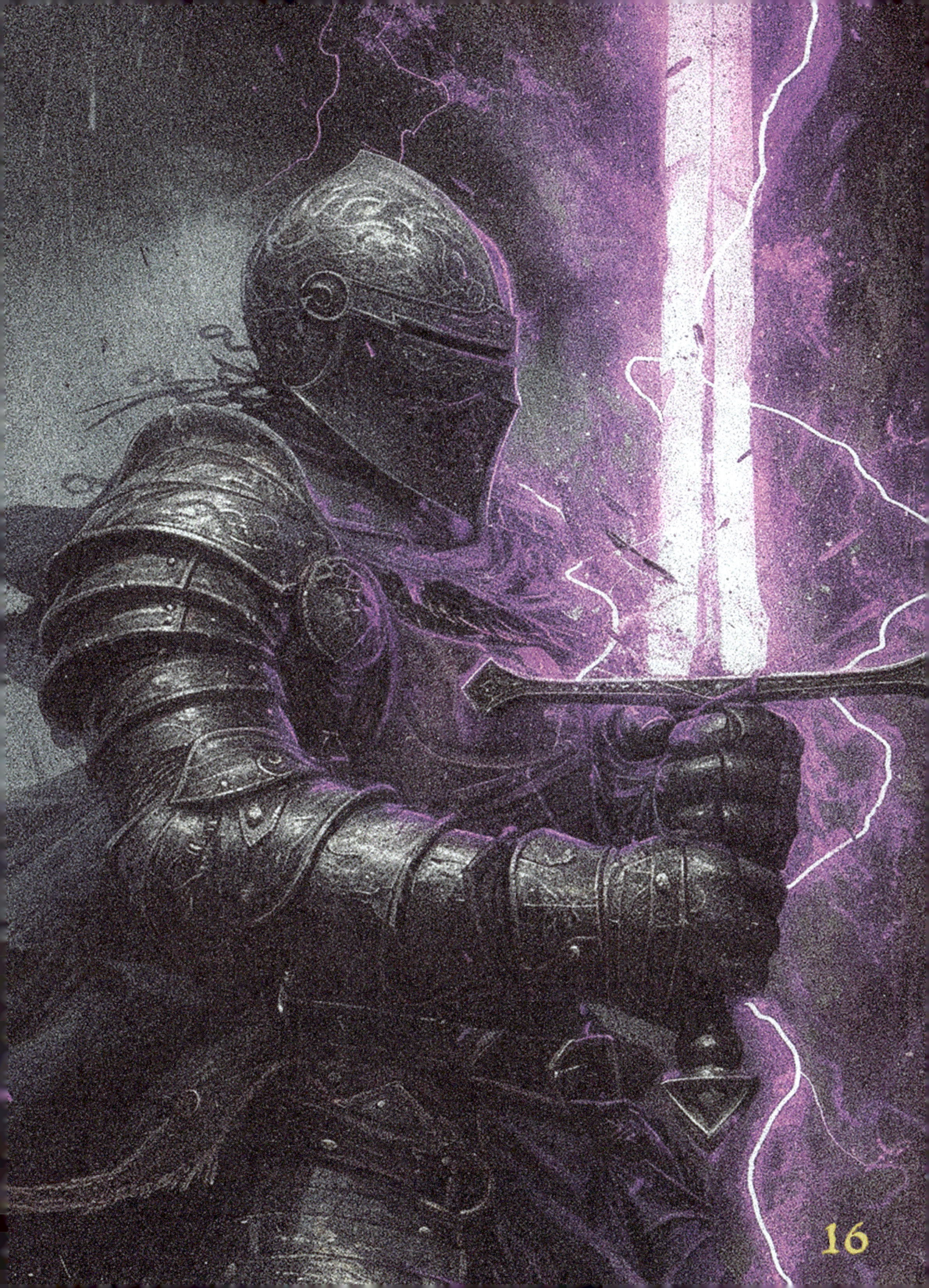

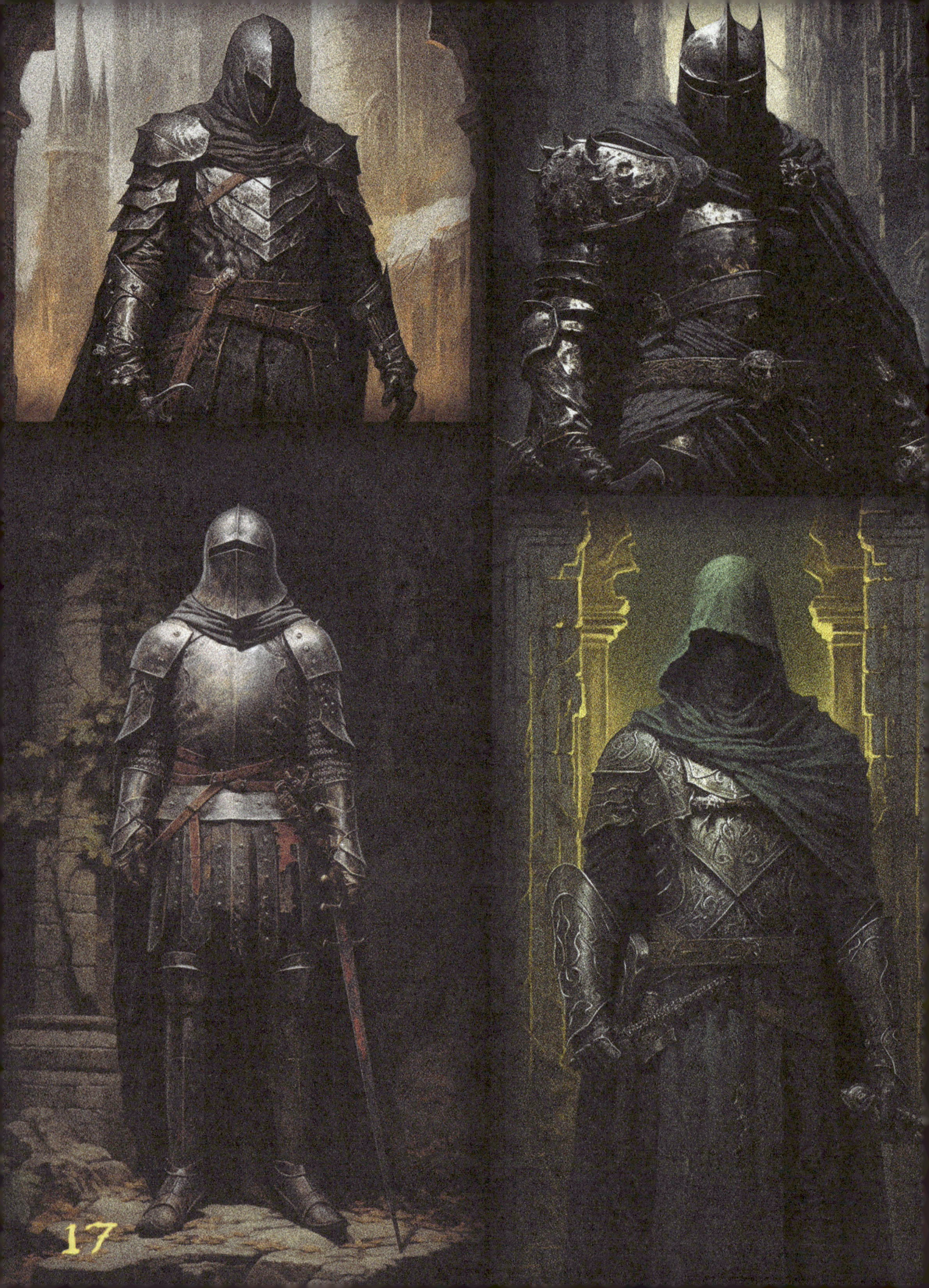

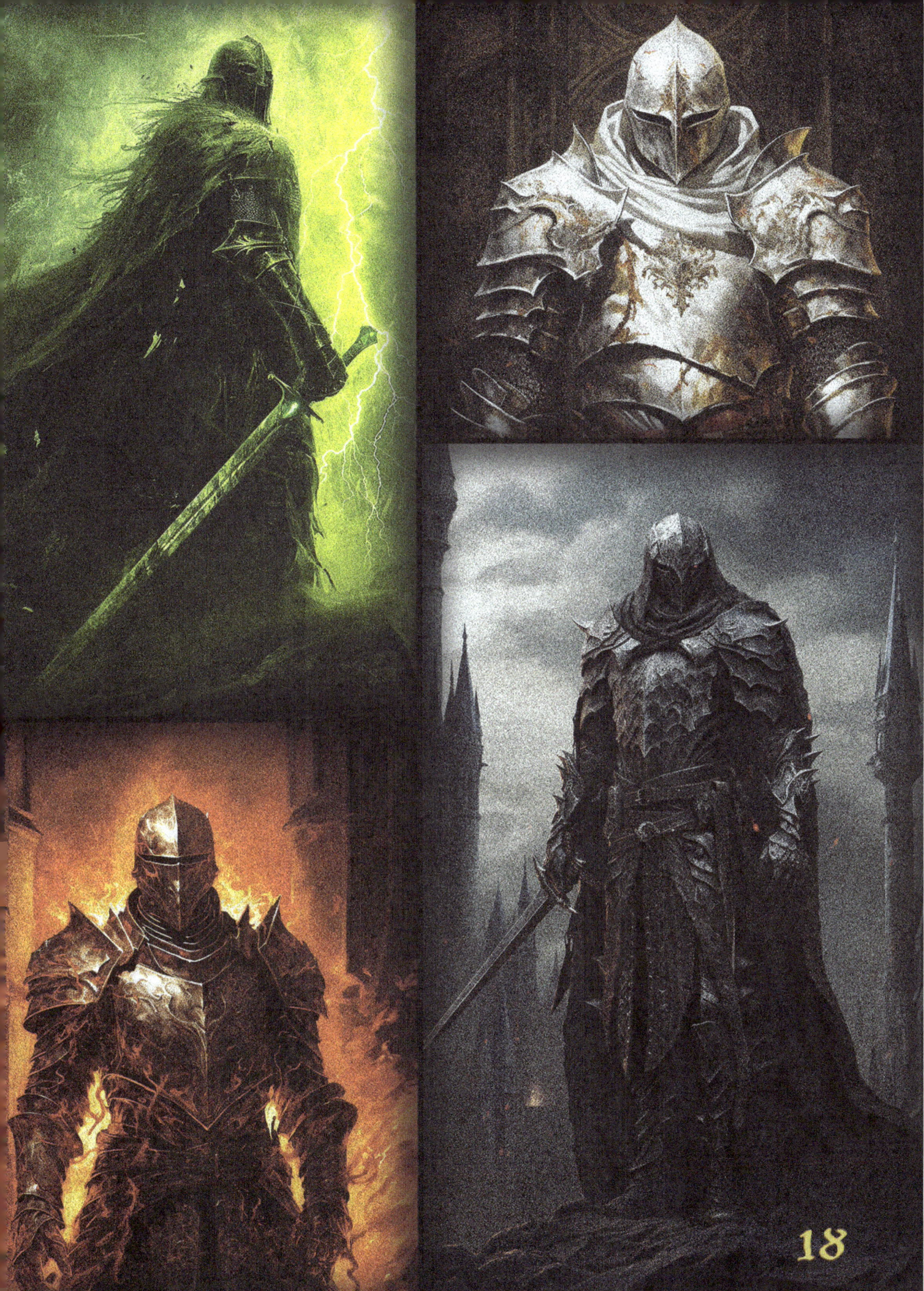

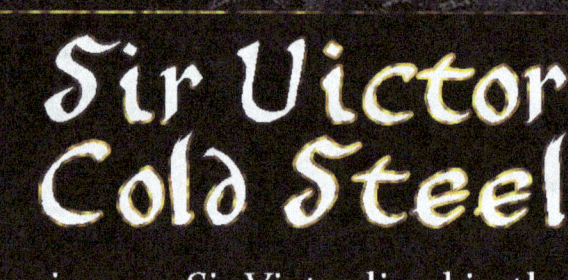

Sir Victor Cold Steel

Growing up, Sir Victor lived in the northern **Cyrofant** city of **Farrendale**. From an early age, he developed an interest in smithing and went on to make his own armour and weapons. His magical ability to meld ice into the steel he wields is what gave him the moniker "Cold Steel." His quests require him to travel frequently through the **Zephyric Regions** in the south, where he enhances his lightning nature magic ability. Sir Victor, though hailing from the **Snowdrift Dominion**, is a close ally to **Thundersgate**. Never truly returning home unless receiving assignments from the lords of **Farrendale**.

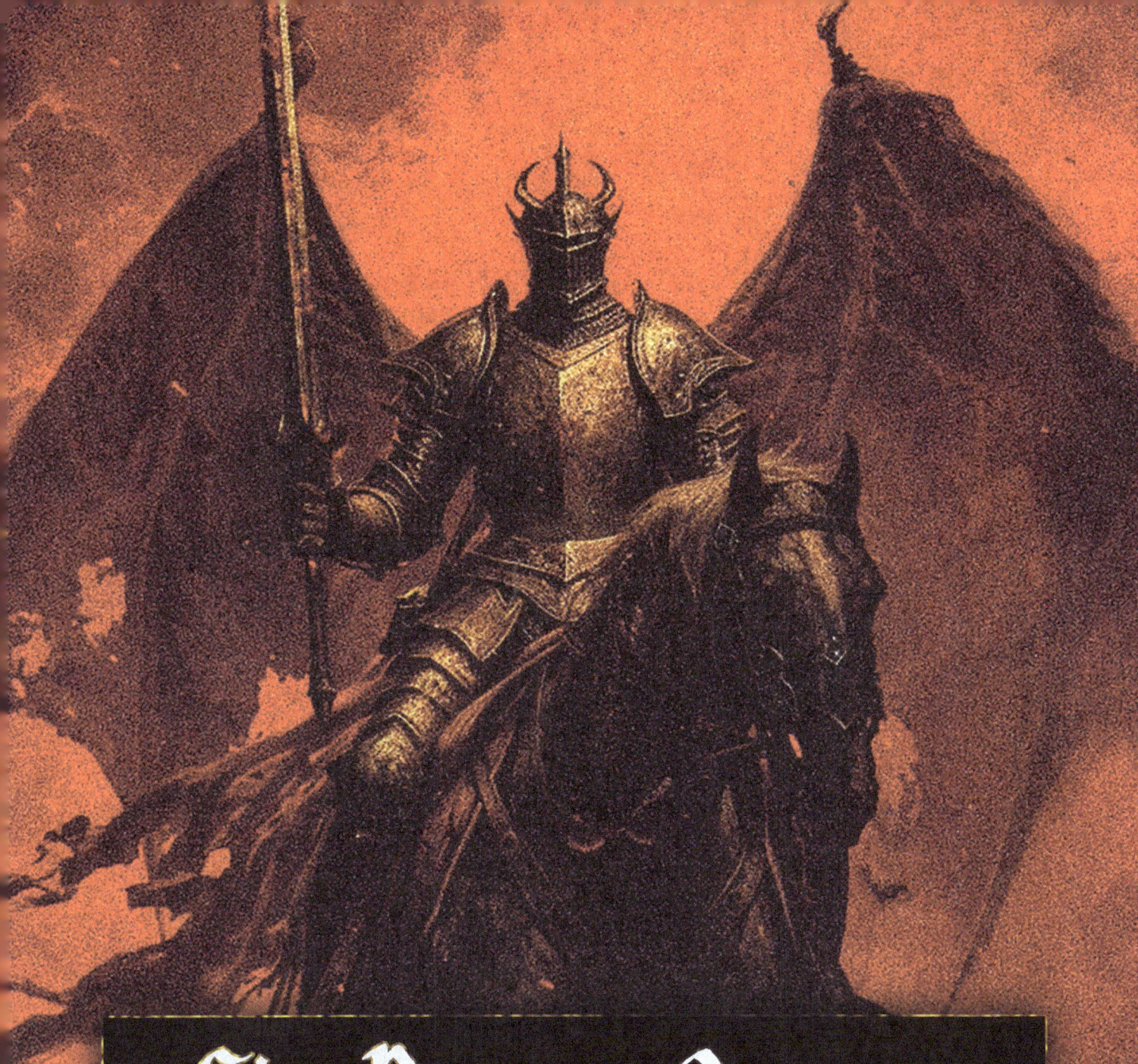

Sir Baron Orwyn

This terrifying knight has surpassed all limits of what was thought natural of an **Eirwynar**. After being kidnapped at a young age he was raised in **Abyssal Reach** of **Bloodmoon Isle**, later being one of the fourteen knighted by **King Morvus Blackthorn** himself. Sir Baron sought more strength by filling his wounds with the flesh of **Imps**, a magical creature that would be the cause of grotesque wings painfully growing from his back. In addition to his formidable mobility, he is a skilled horse rider and possesses longsword and pole-arm mastery.

Thieves

Gwyn has a vast network of thieves and mercenaries all spread throughout the realm, all holding allegiances and all having sworn enemies. Theft is an art that is rarely practised in the eyes of the general public; it is a behaviour that is despised and mistrusted by many. Though many of the best thieves end up being valuable assets to their kingdoms because of their skill at detection and stealth.

Poison brewing and illusion magic are common practices among thieves. Many who adopt this lifestyle are sworn in with a code known as the **Pledge of Liars** and are then branded with a sigil of their home region on the palms of both hands.

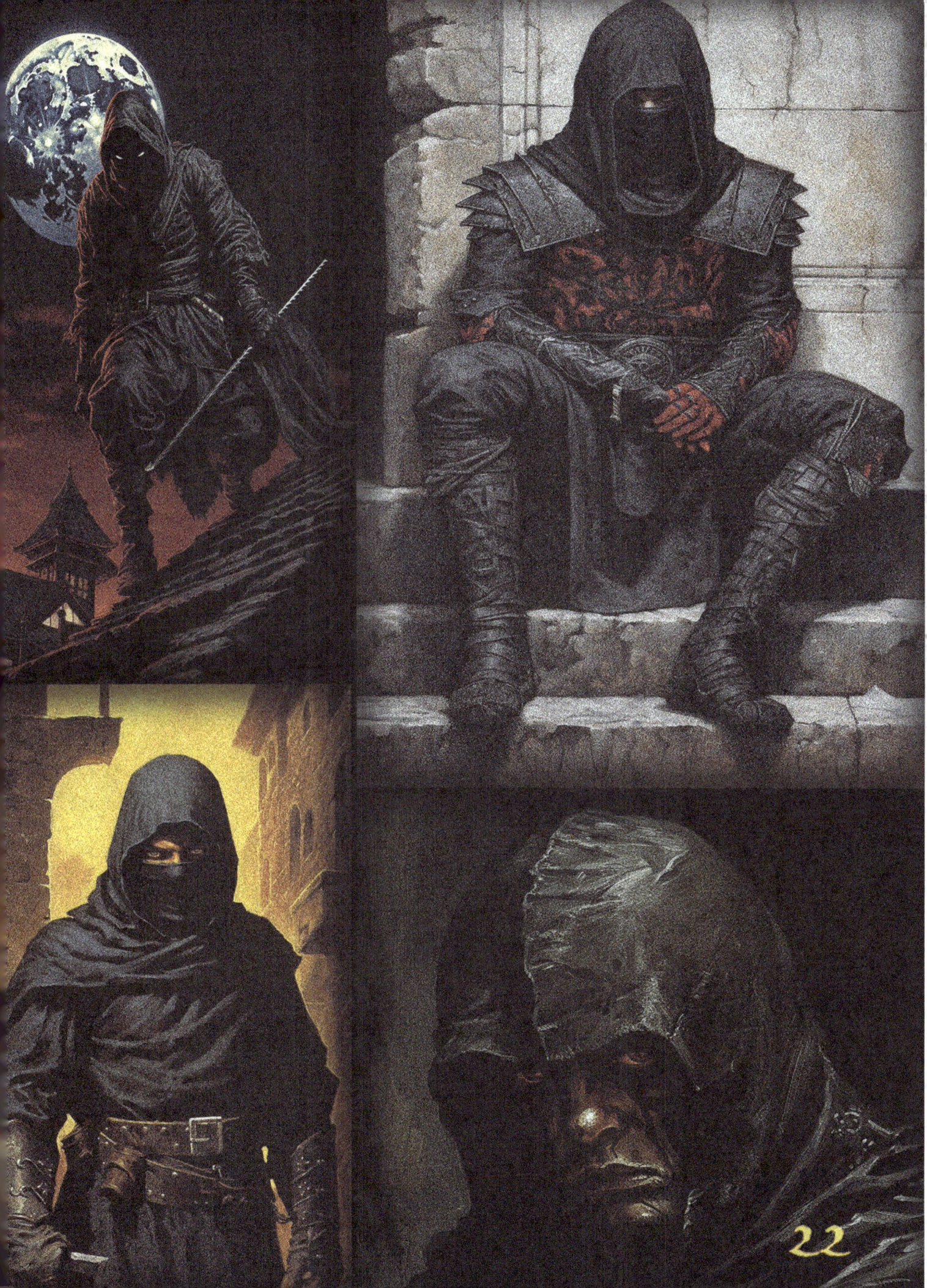

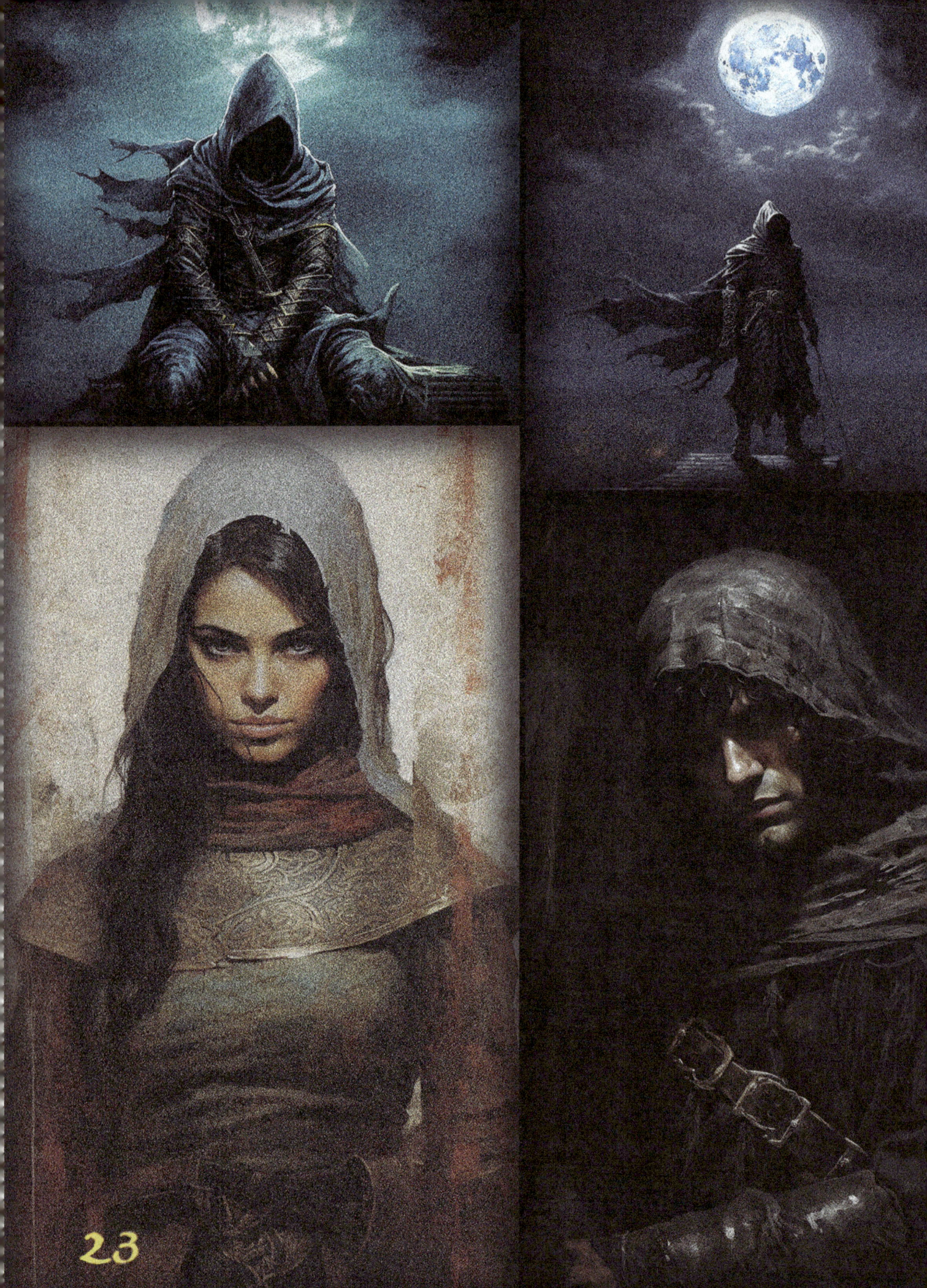

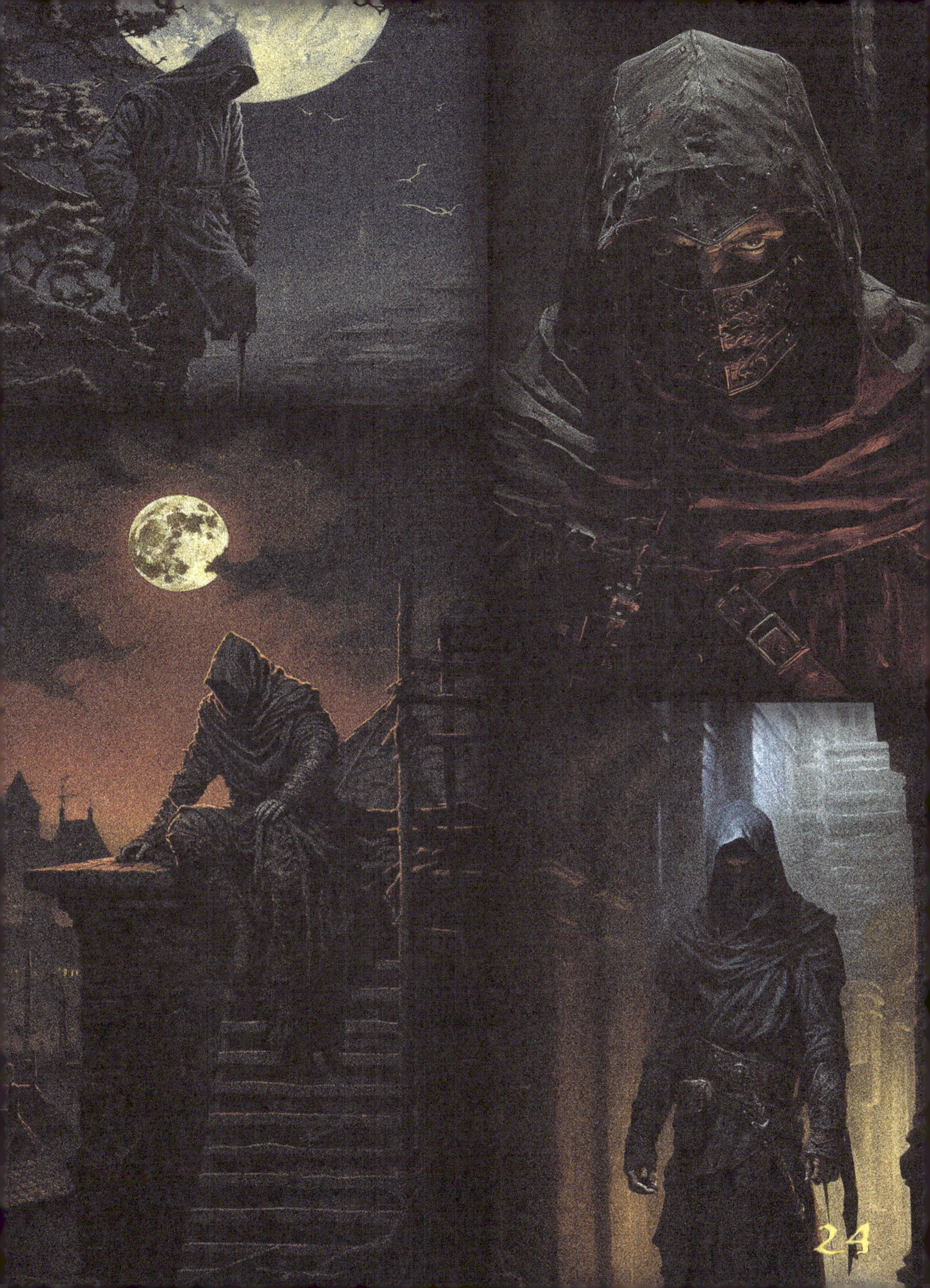

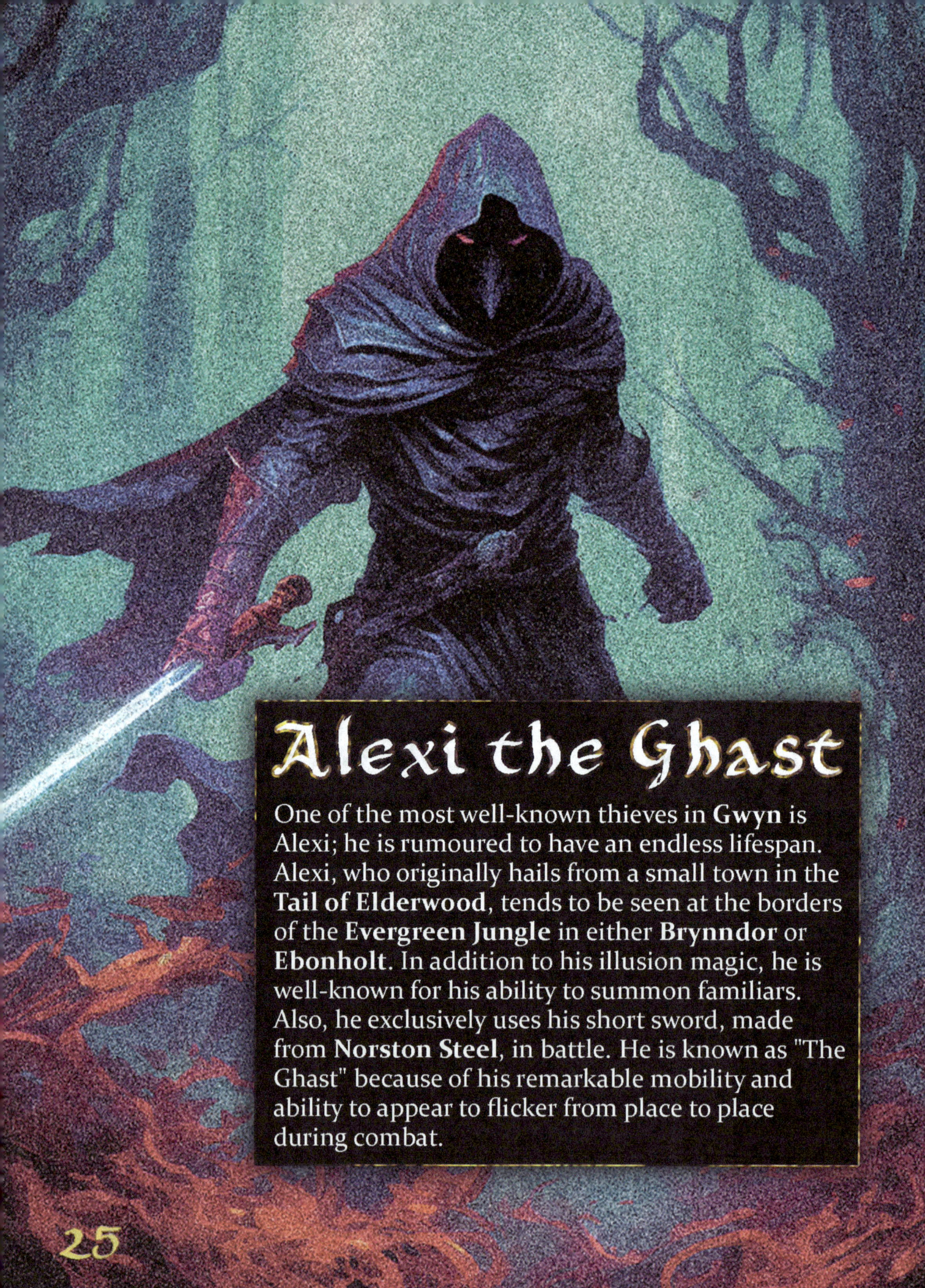

Alexi the Ghast

One of the most well-known thieves in **Gwyn** is Alexi; he is rumoured to have an endless lifespan. Alexi, who originally hails from a small town in the **Tail of Elderwood**, tends to be seen at the borders of the **Evergreen Jungle** in either **Brynndor** or **Ebonholt**. In addition to his illusion magic, he is well-known for his ability to summon familiars. Also, he exclusively uses his short sword, made from **Norston Steel**, in battle. He is known as "The Ghast" because of his remarkable mobility and ability to appear to flicker from place to place during combat.

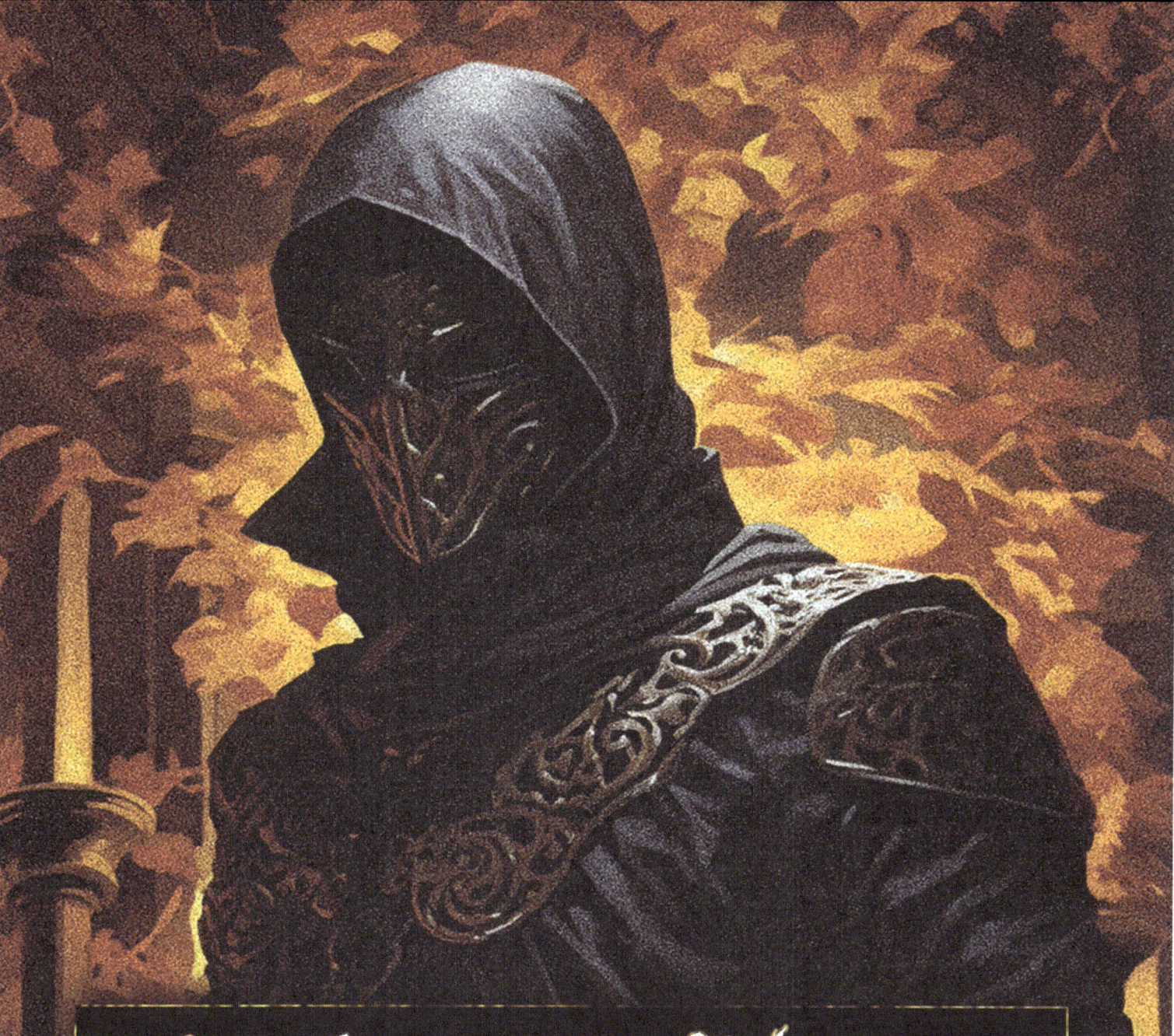

Eoghan of Silence

This thief, who is from the **Zephyric Region** of **Tarranon**, has avoided public attention his entire life. He is only known for his purple clothing and golden armour. Eoghan is one of the few thieves who prefers to use a longsword as his primary hand weapon, but his true skill is poisoning. When seen, he is known as "Silence". Since mass poisoning deaths frequently follow his sightings, he has taken on the traits of an urban legend.

"Beware the shadow's tread, for where Silence roams, death is led."

Regions

Gwyn

The realm of **Gwyn** comprises of five unique countries and an alignment of six gods; **Maelgor, Cyfandor, Zephyrus, Seraphina, Gwiraelin**, and **Eldorin**. They watch over a diverse array of inhabitants and landscapes. The five countries are **Bloodmoon Isle** under **King Morvus Blackthorn, Ebonholt** ruled by **Queen Zephyra Darkfyre, Brynndor** held by the democratic **Arcane Sovereign Guild, The Snowdrift Dominion** led by **King Bore Icemane**, and **Rhyddia** presided over by **Queen Elwen Aurandor**.

Stormspear

Tarranon

Derwenholt

Twilight Citadel

Elderwood

Greenbriar

Brynndor

Brynndor is geographically divided into two distinct halves. The southern **Seraphiric Region** is characterised by its lower altitude, featuring green, rolling hills and expansive meadows. This region is filled with dense woodland areas, all infused with the essence of **Seraphina** and being where the capital is located, **Twilight Citadel**. The northern **Zephyric Region** of **Brynndor** is defined by a high-altitude mountain range, where clouds and thunder are prevalent. The mountains vary in height, gradually reaching their highest near the border of the **Snowdrift Dominion** (north). This part of **Brynndor** holds the essence of **Zephyrus**. **Brynndor** has five separate kingdoms, **Stormspear**, **Tarannon**, **Derwenholt**, **Elderwood**, and **Greenbriar**.

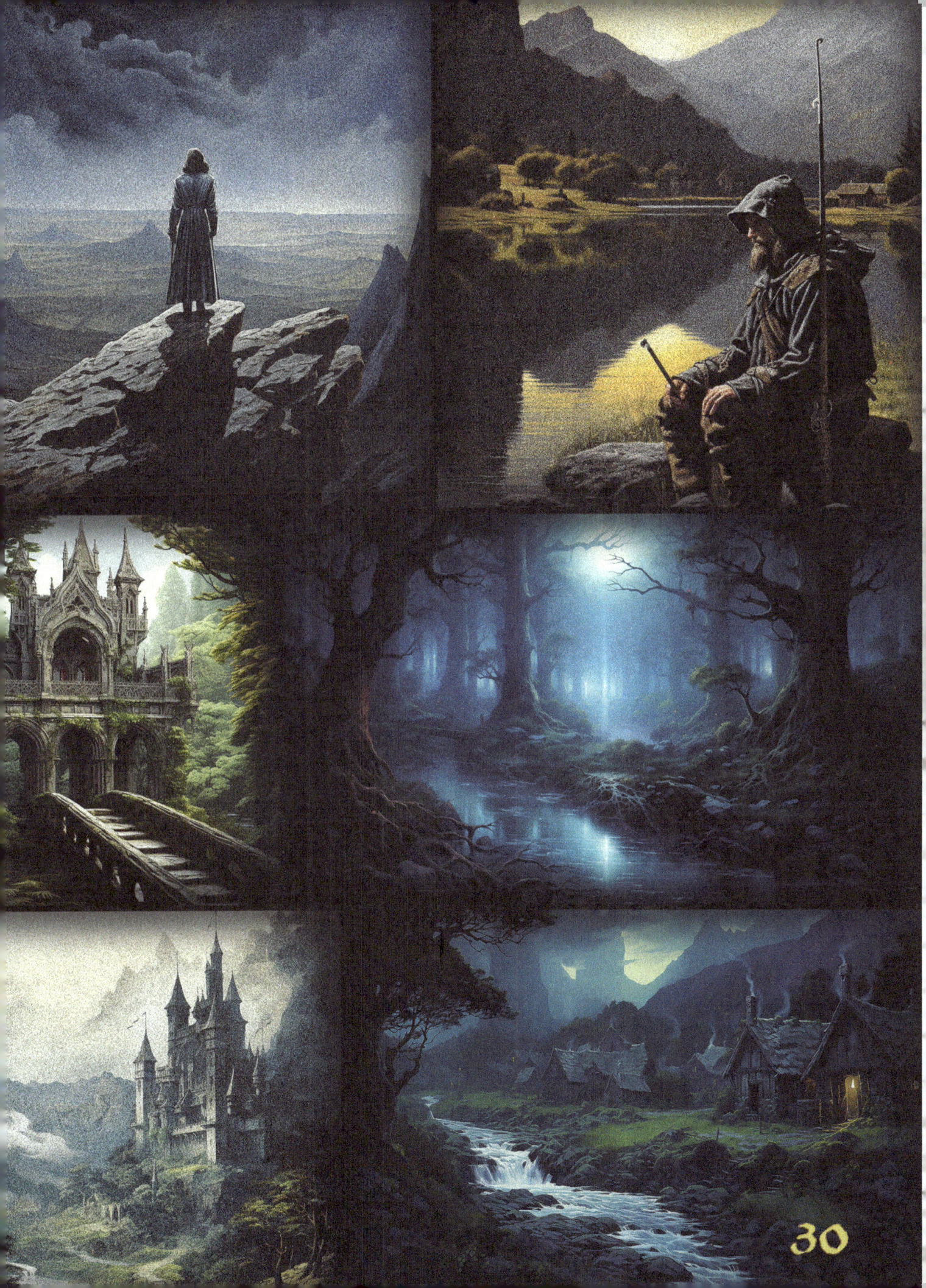

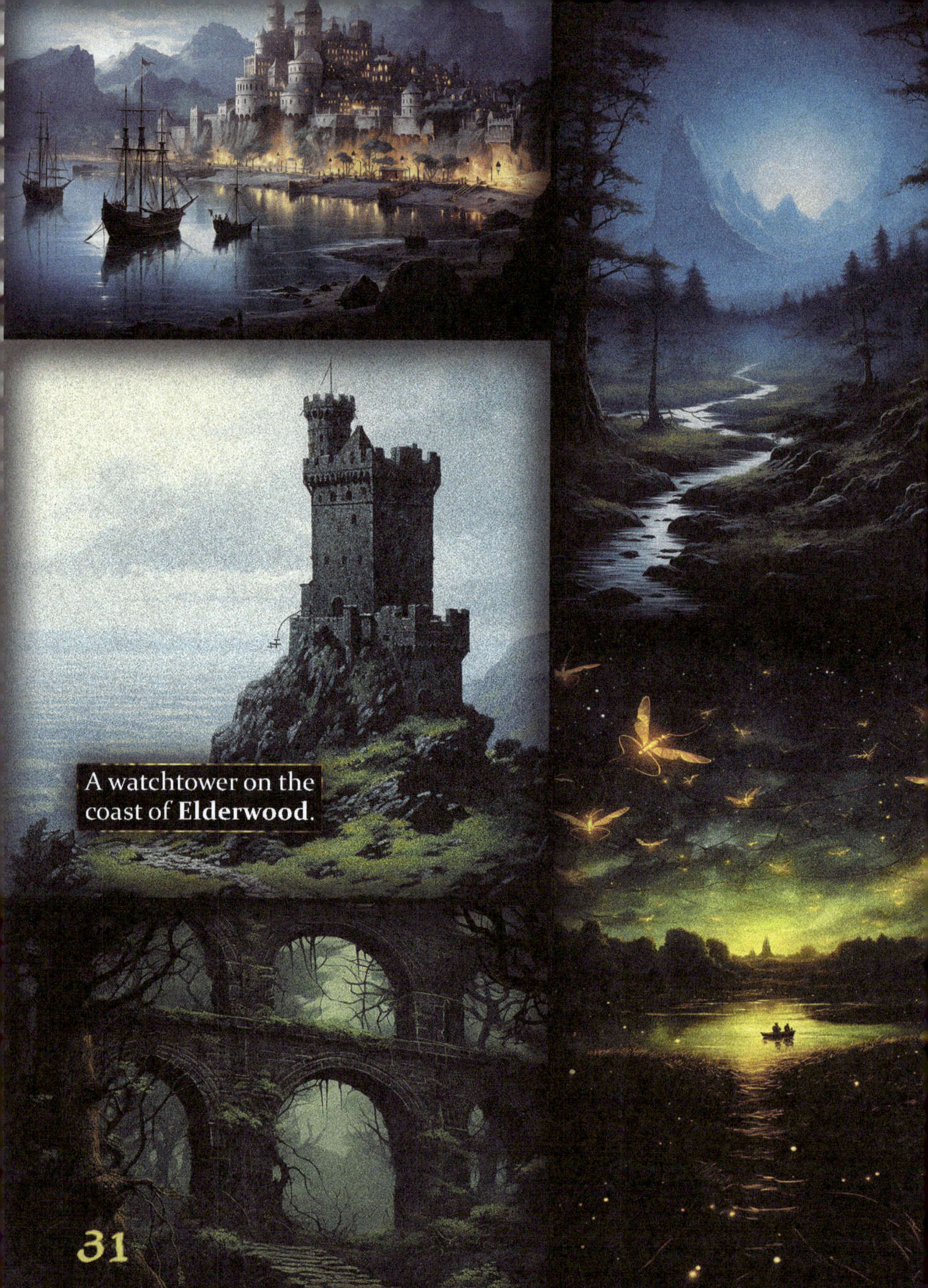

A watchtower on the coast of **Elderwood**.

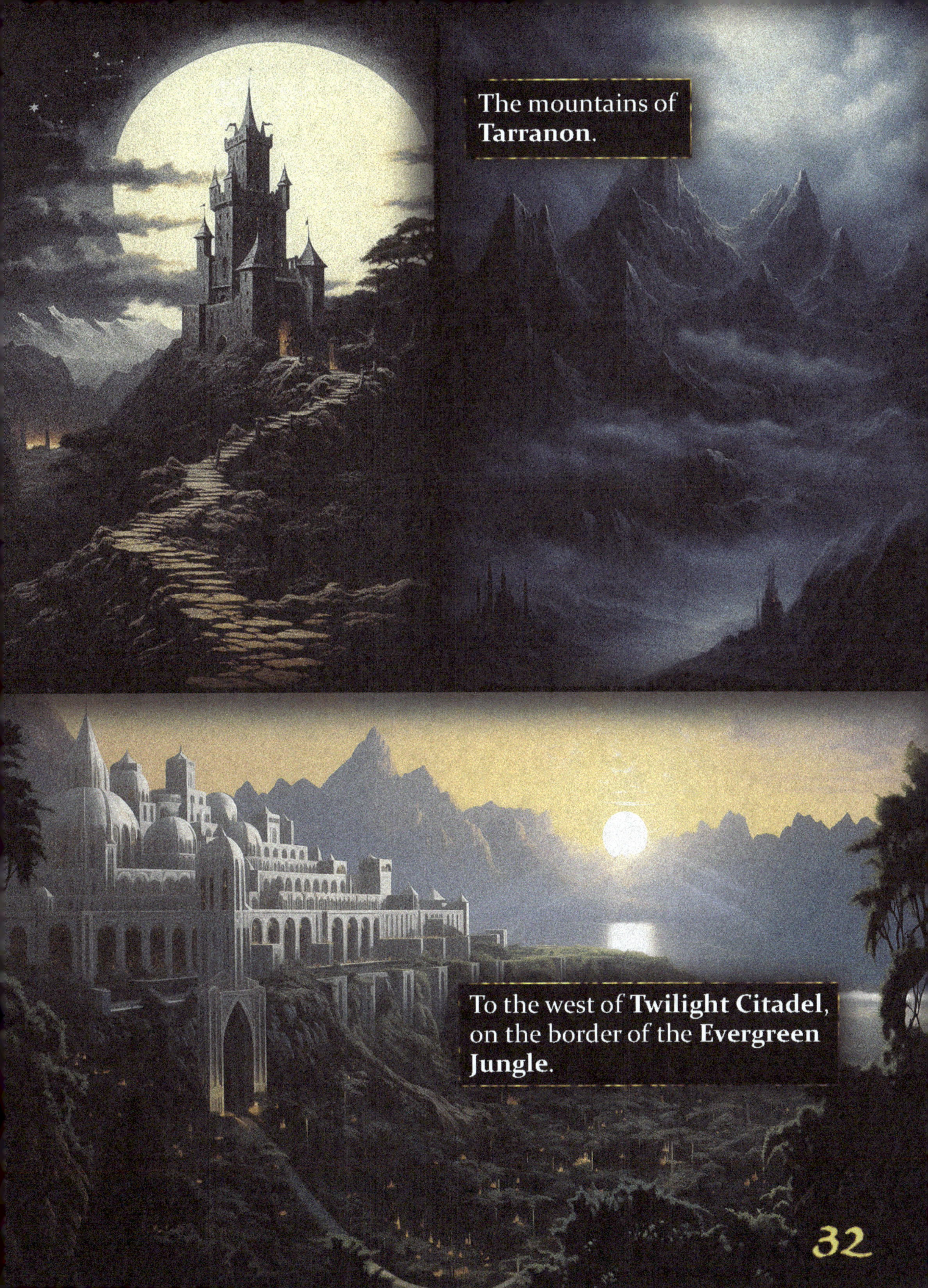

Twilight Citadel

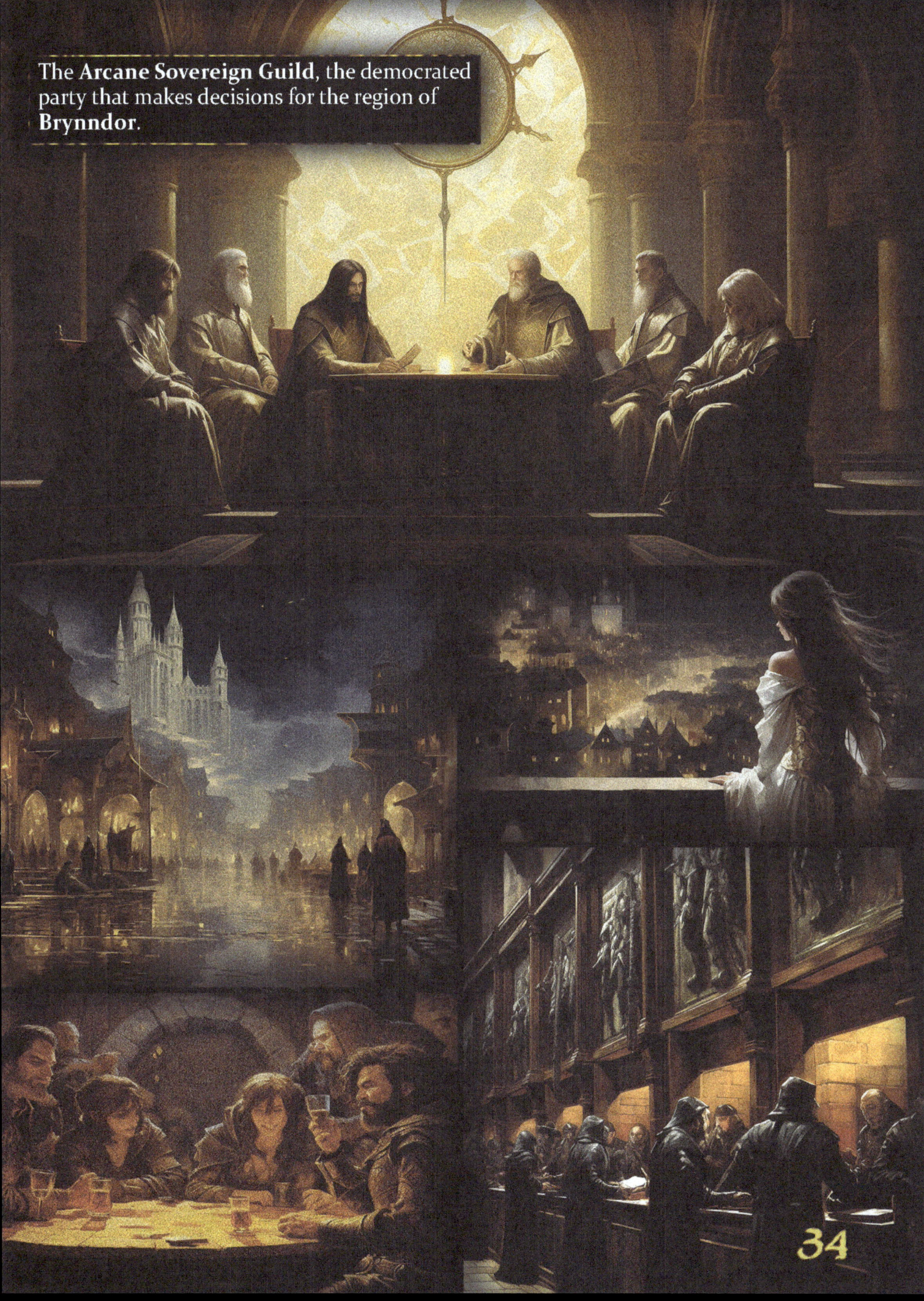

The **Arcane Sovereign Guild**, the democrated party that makes decisions for the region of **Brynndor**.

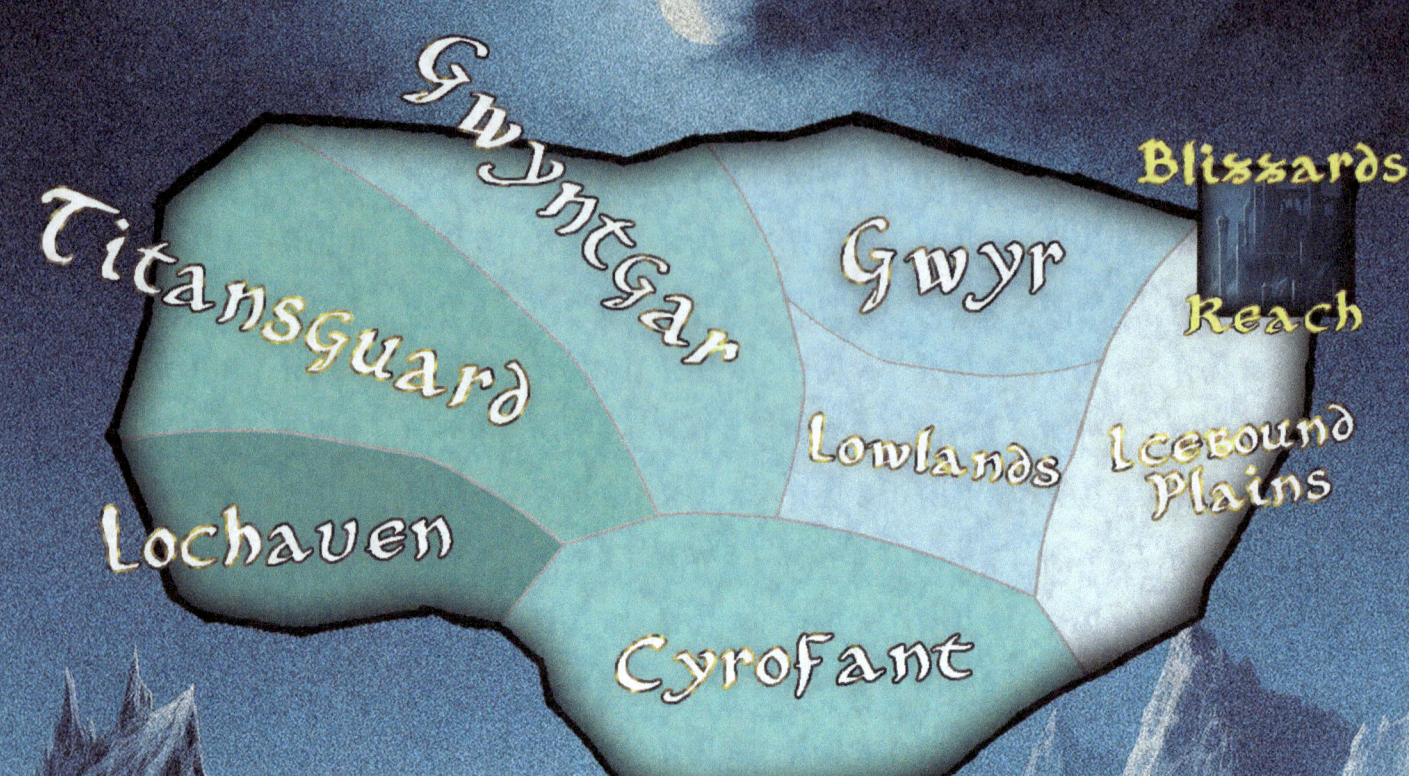

Snowdrift Dominion

The Snowdrift Dominion is a cold, snowy land where the **Titanborn** live. It's harsh most of the year, and it holds ancient artefacts and resources from the past. The land is rich with the essence of the gods due to the enduring cold weather. The **Snowdrift Dominion** consists of seven regions: **Cyrofant**, **Lochaven**, **Titansguard**, **Gwyntgar**, **Gwyr**, the **Lowlands**, and the **Icebound Plains**. The capital, **Blizzards Reach**, is located in the **Icebound Plains**, completely surrounded by the coast. There is a strong alliance within the **Snowdrift Dominion** that provides the continent with rich resources and infrastructure, called the **Ice Forged Confederacy**, this is made up of **Lochaven**, **Titansguard**, and **Gwyntgar**.

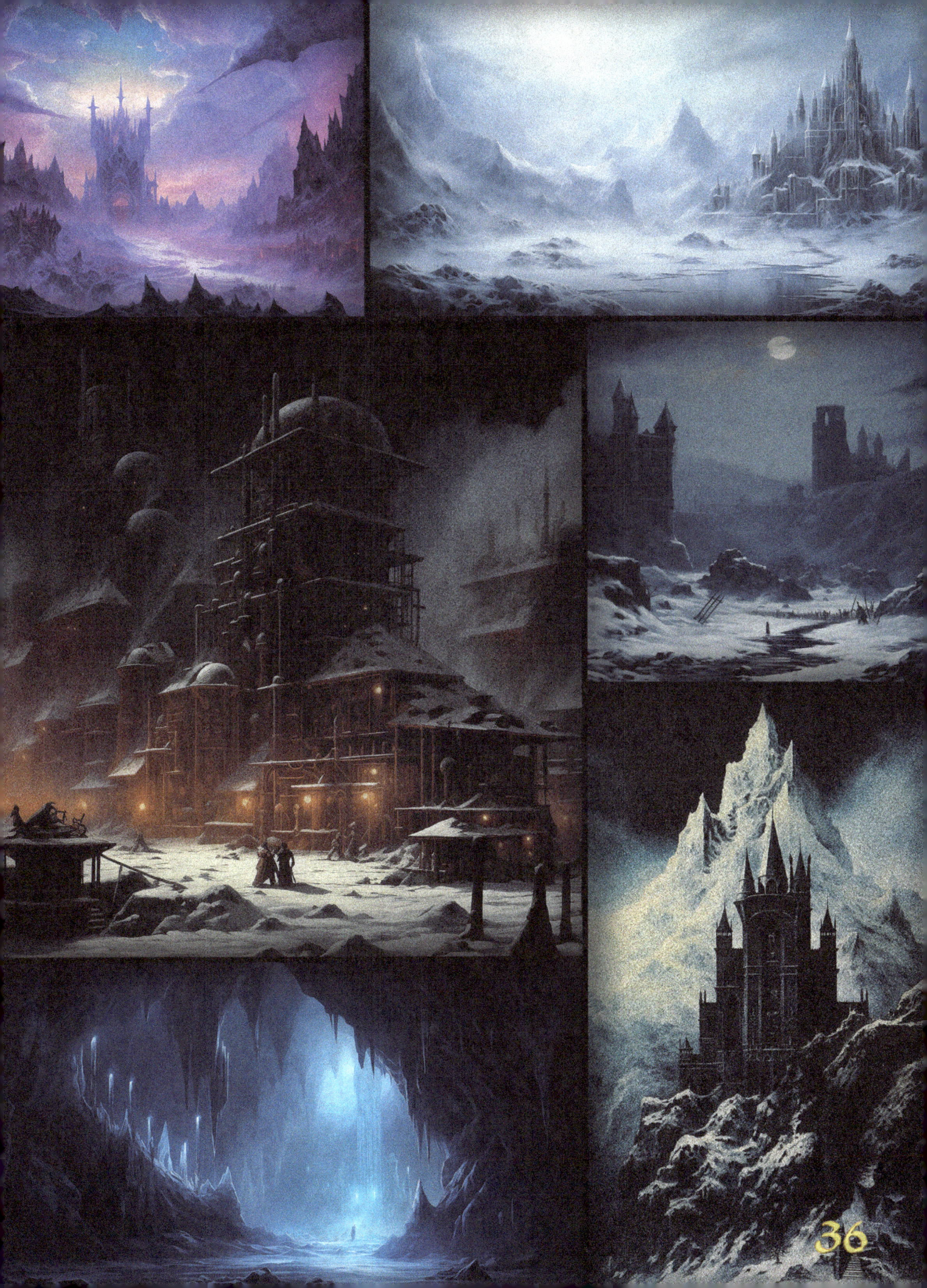

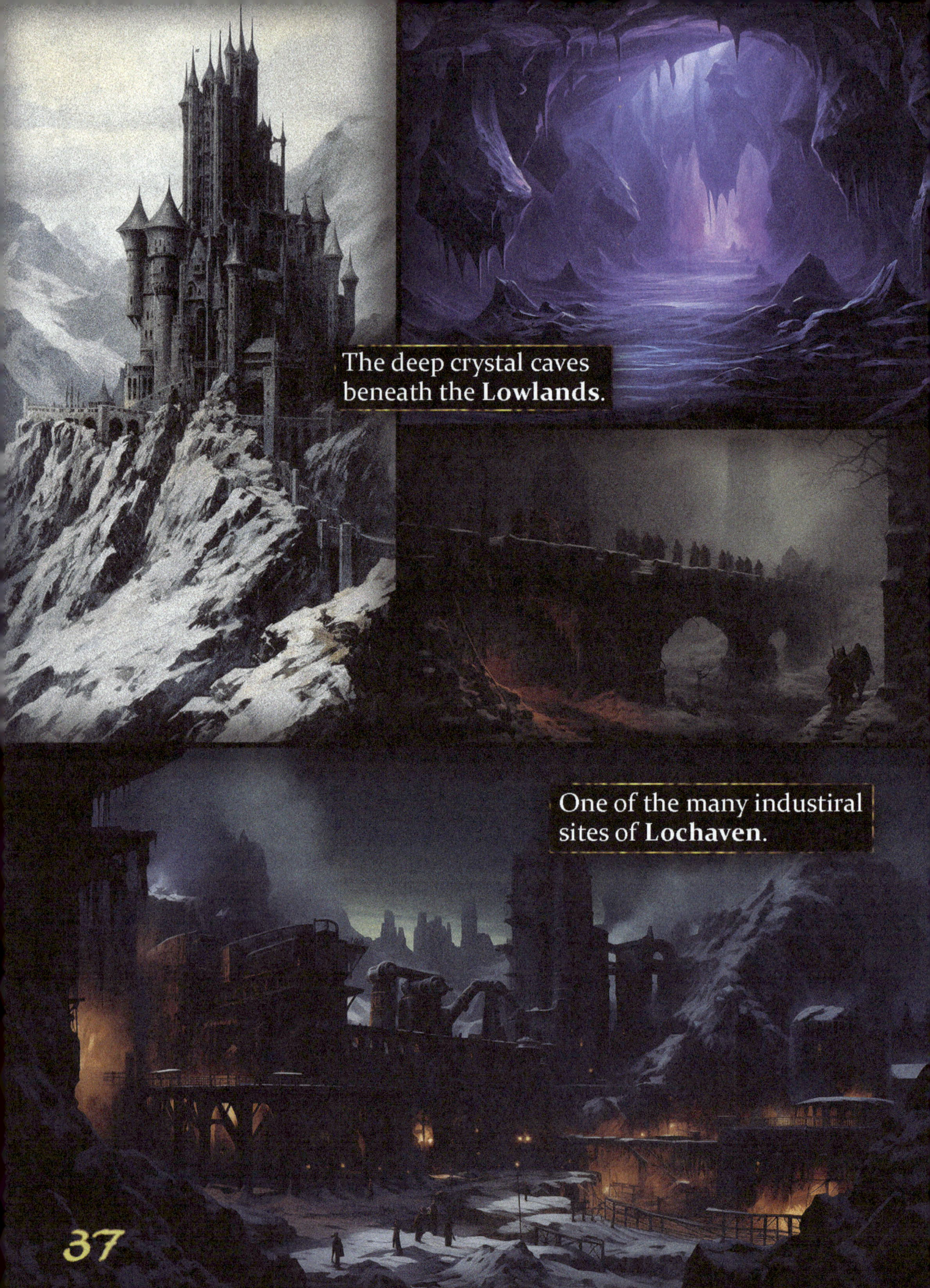

The deep crystal caves beneath the **Lowlands**.

One of the many industiral sites of **Lochaven**.

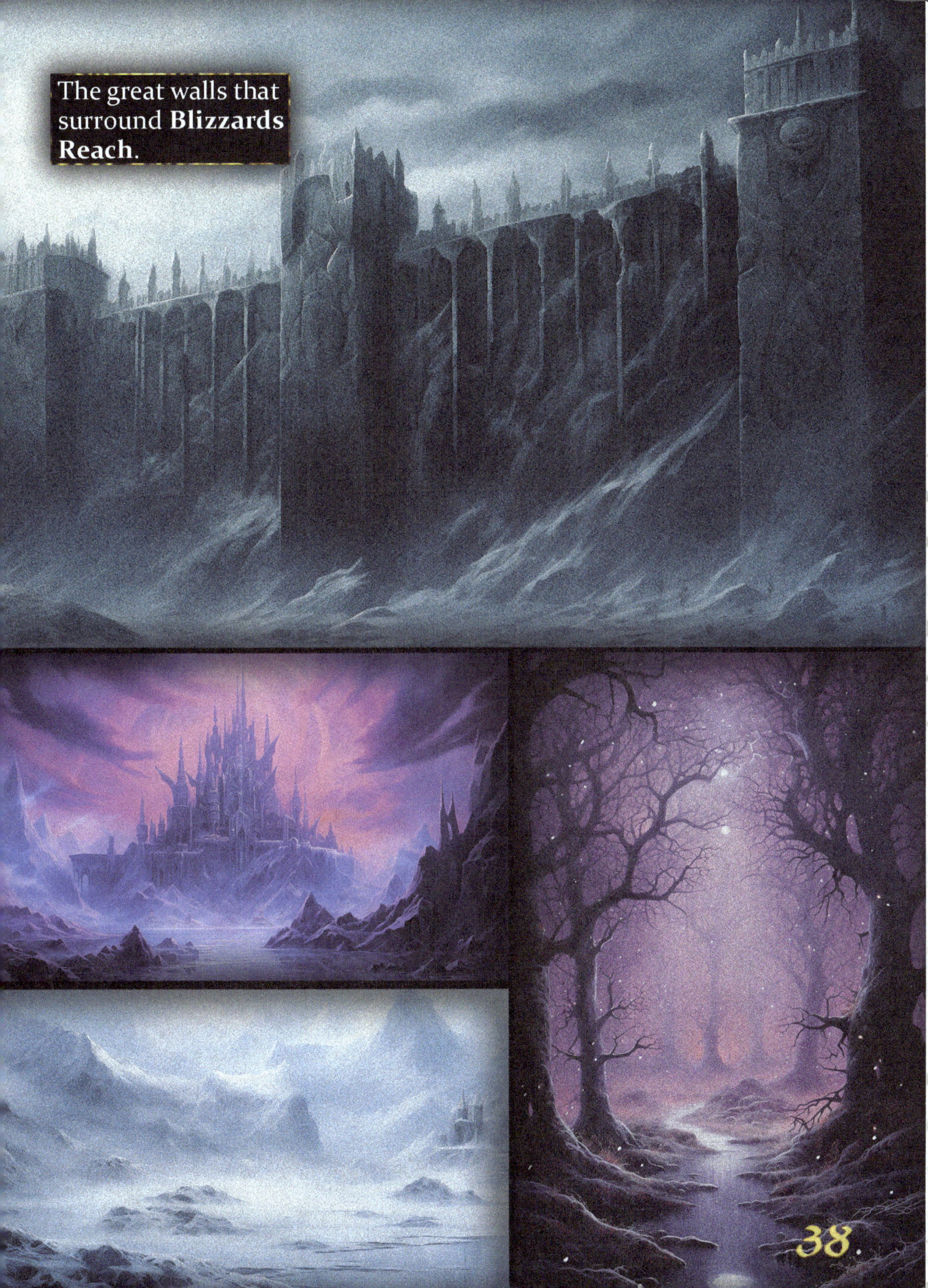

The great walls that surround **Blizzards Reach**.

Blizzards Reach

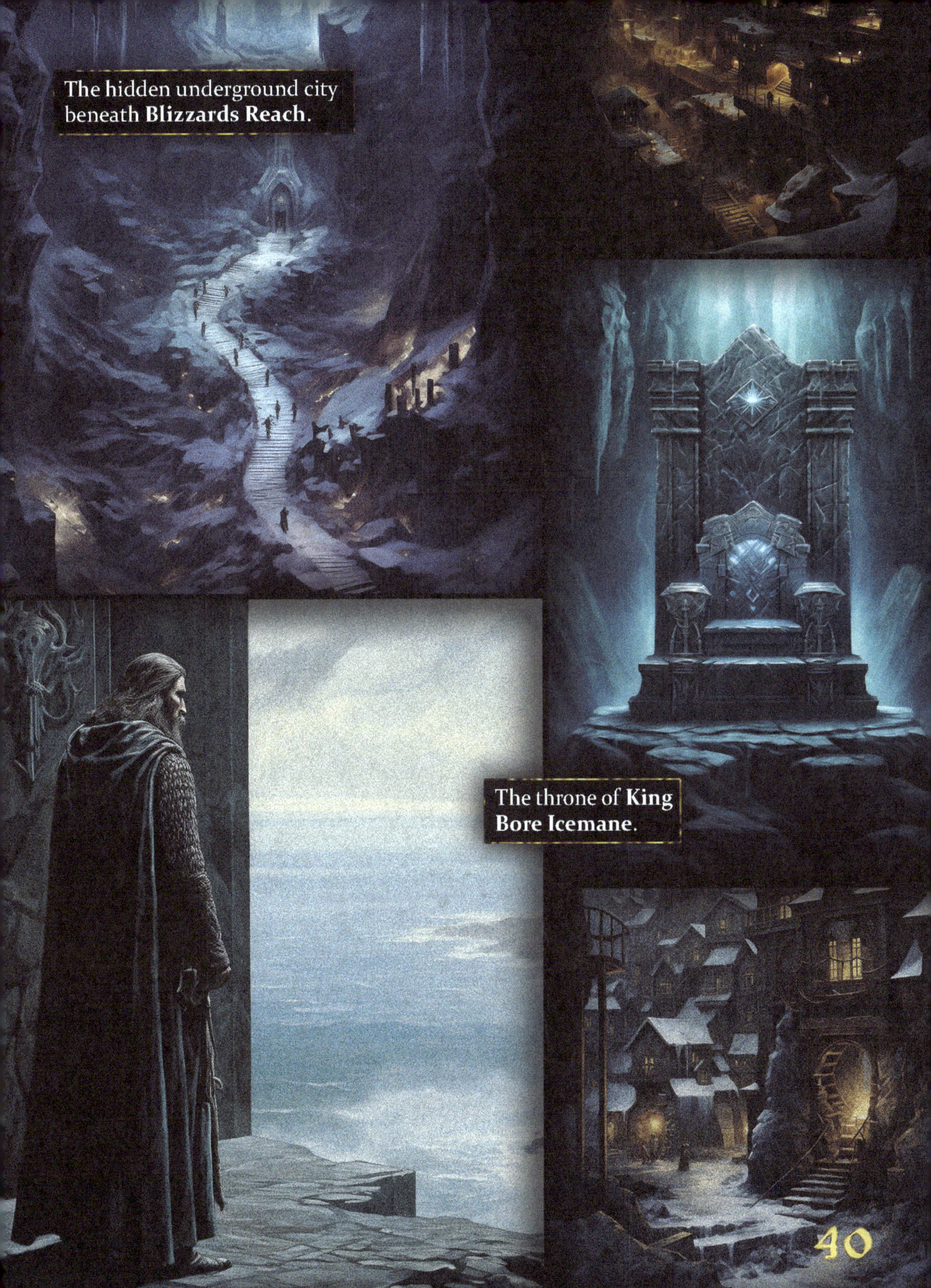

The hidden underground city beneath **Blizzards Reach**.

The throne of **King Bore Icemane**.

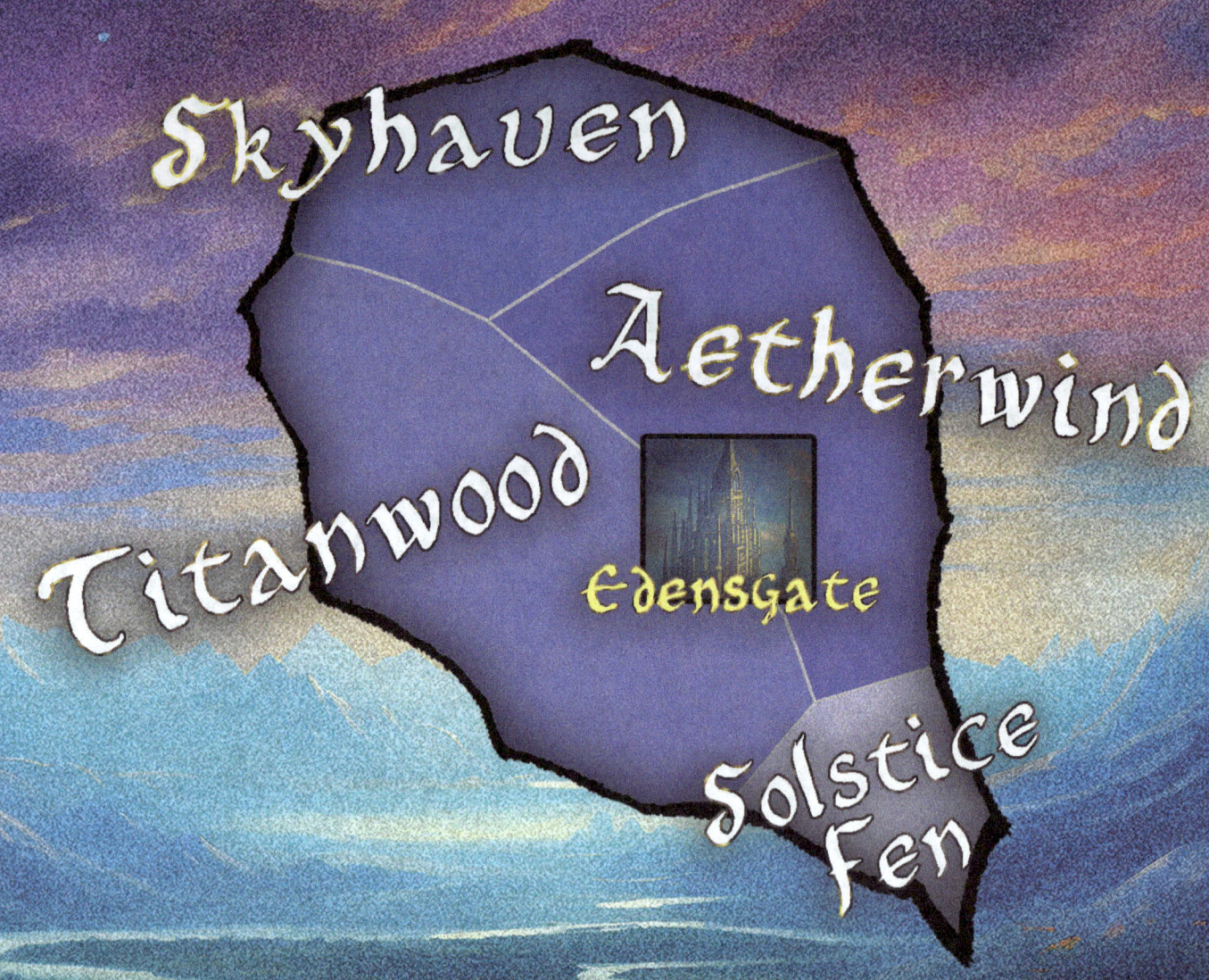

Rhyddia

Rhyddia is a mystical area where water is a key element. In the north, it's windy with rocky terrain featuring blue, crystal-like veins in the stones. The west boasts a large forest of unique dark brown and blue oak trees, home to many mystical creatures. Around the capital, **Edensgate**, the climate is calmer, while the south is barren and the resting place for **The Abysswatcher** once a year. **Rhyddia** consists of four regions: **Skyhaven**, **Aetherwind**, **Titanwood**, and **Solstice Fen**, each embodying the essence of Eldorin.

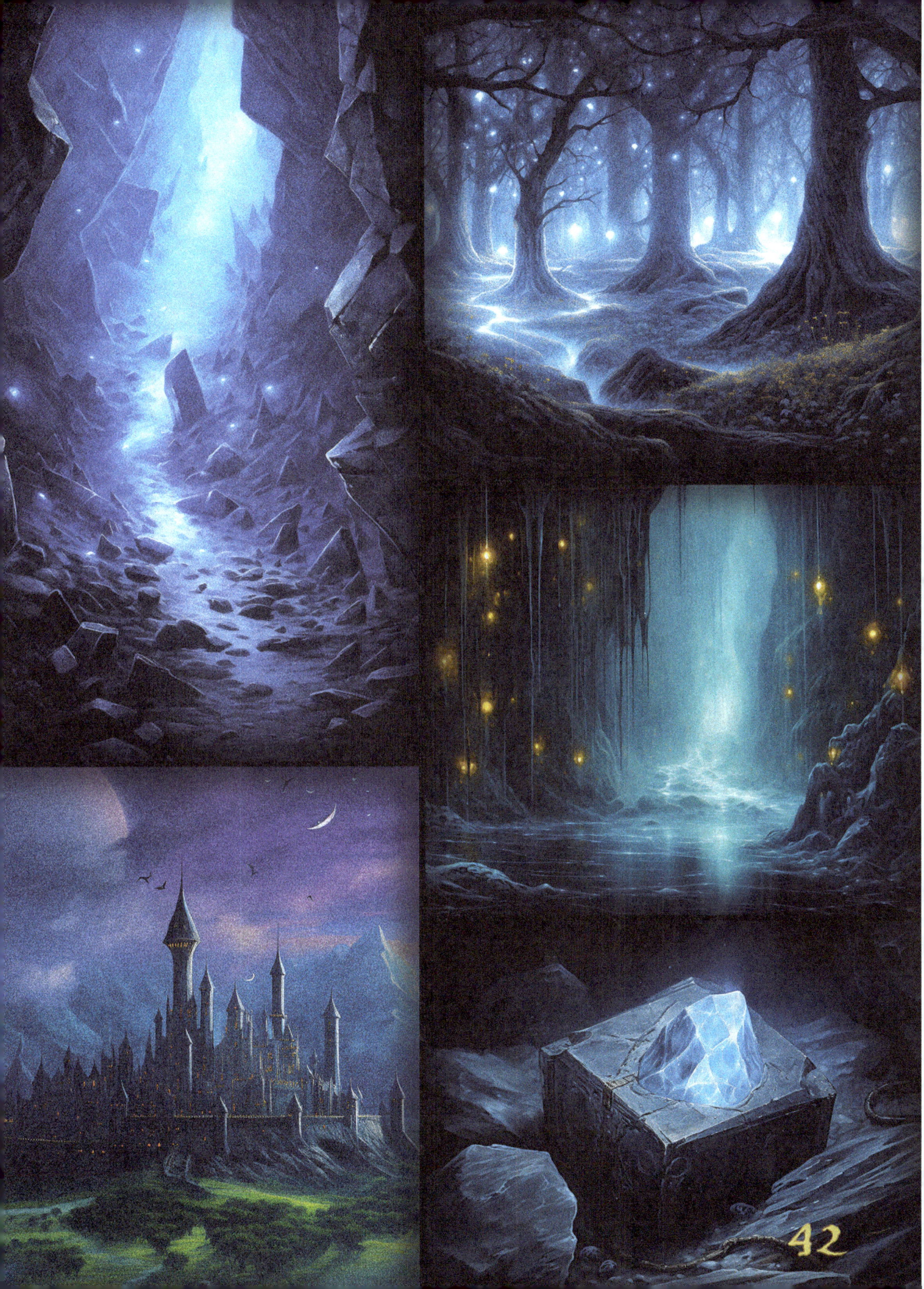

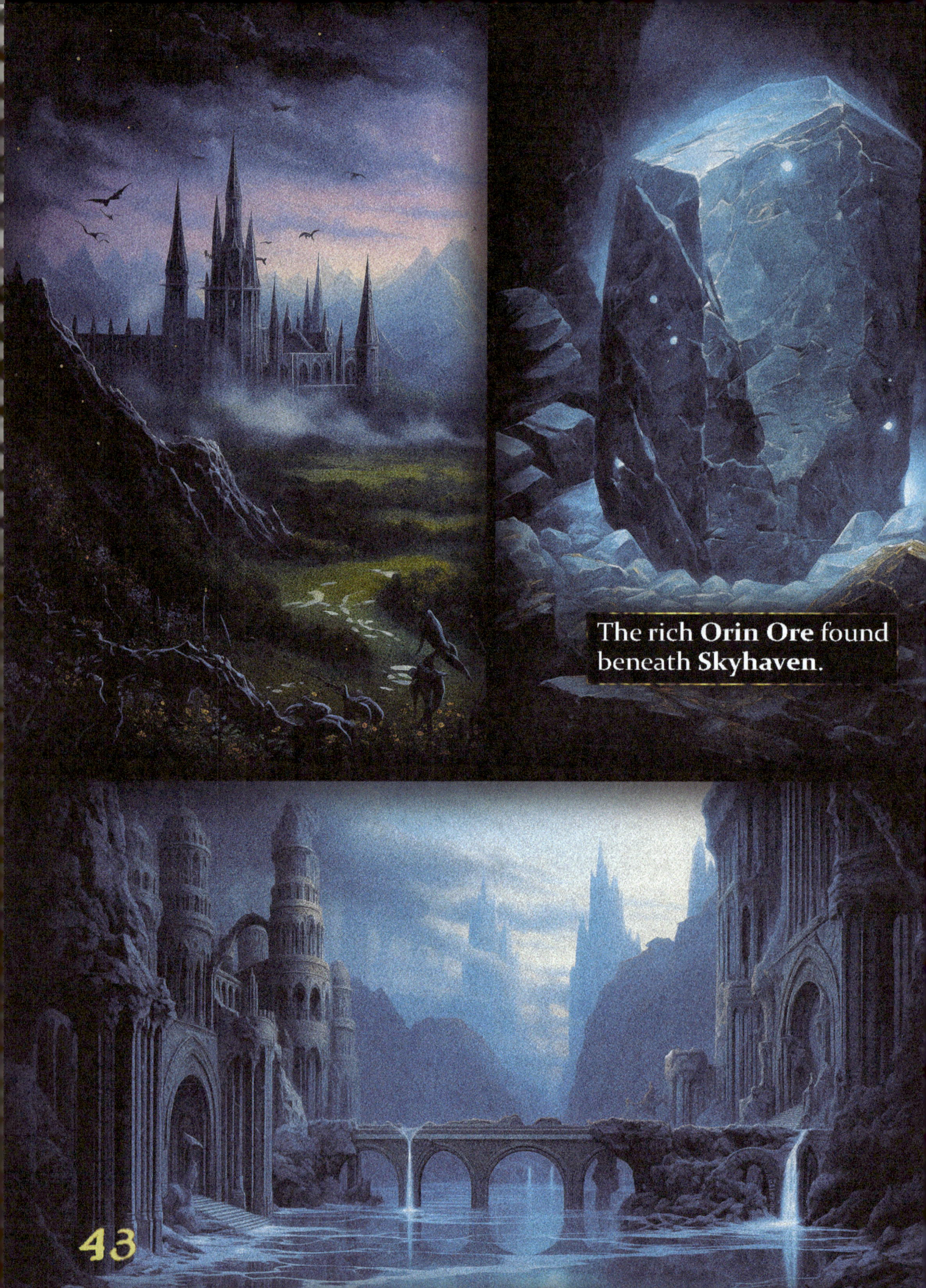

The rich **Orin Ore** found beneath **Skyhaven**.

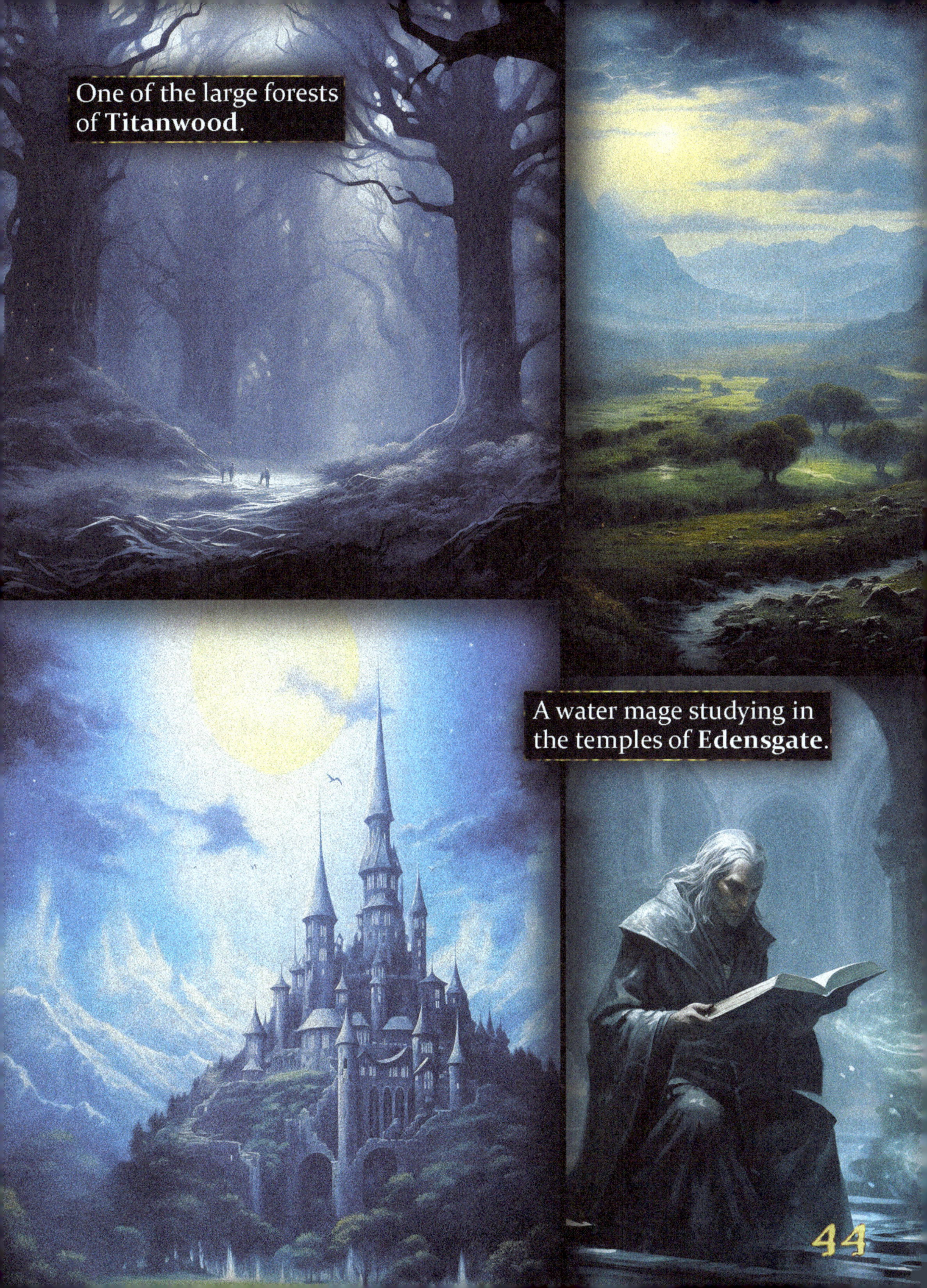

One of the large forests of **Titanwood**.

A water mage studying in the temples of **Edensgate**.

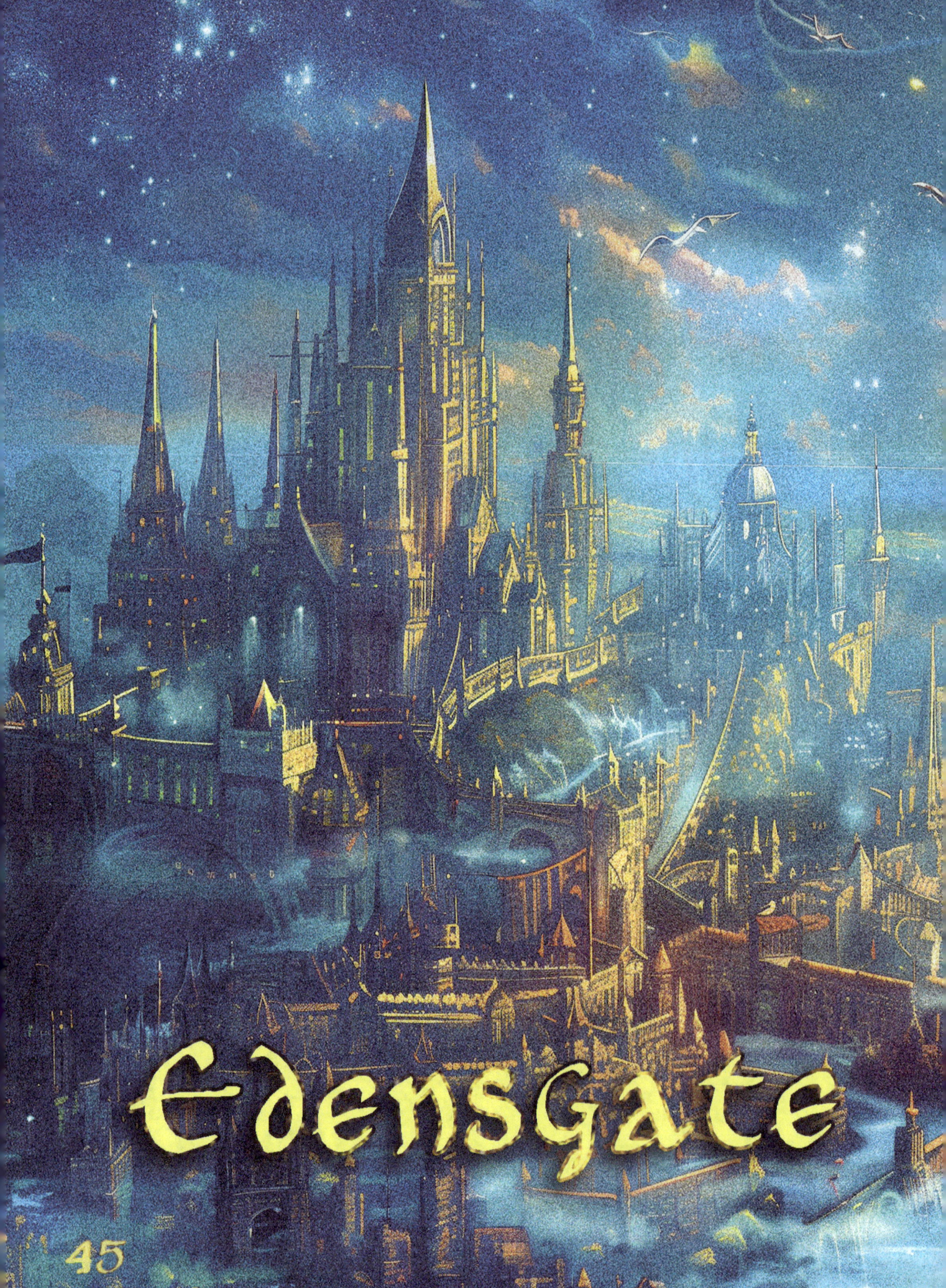

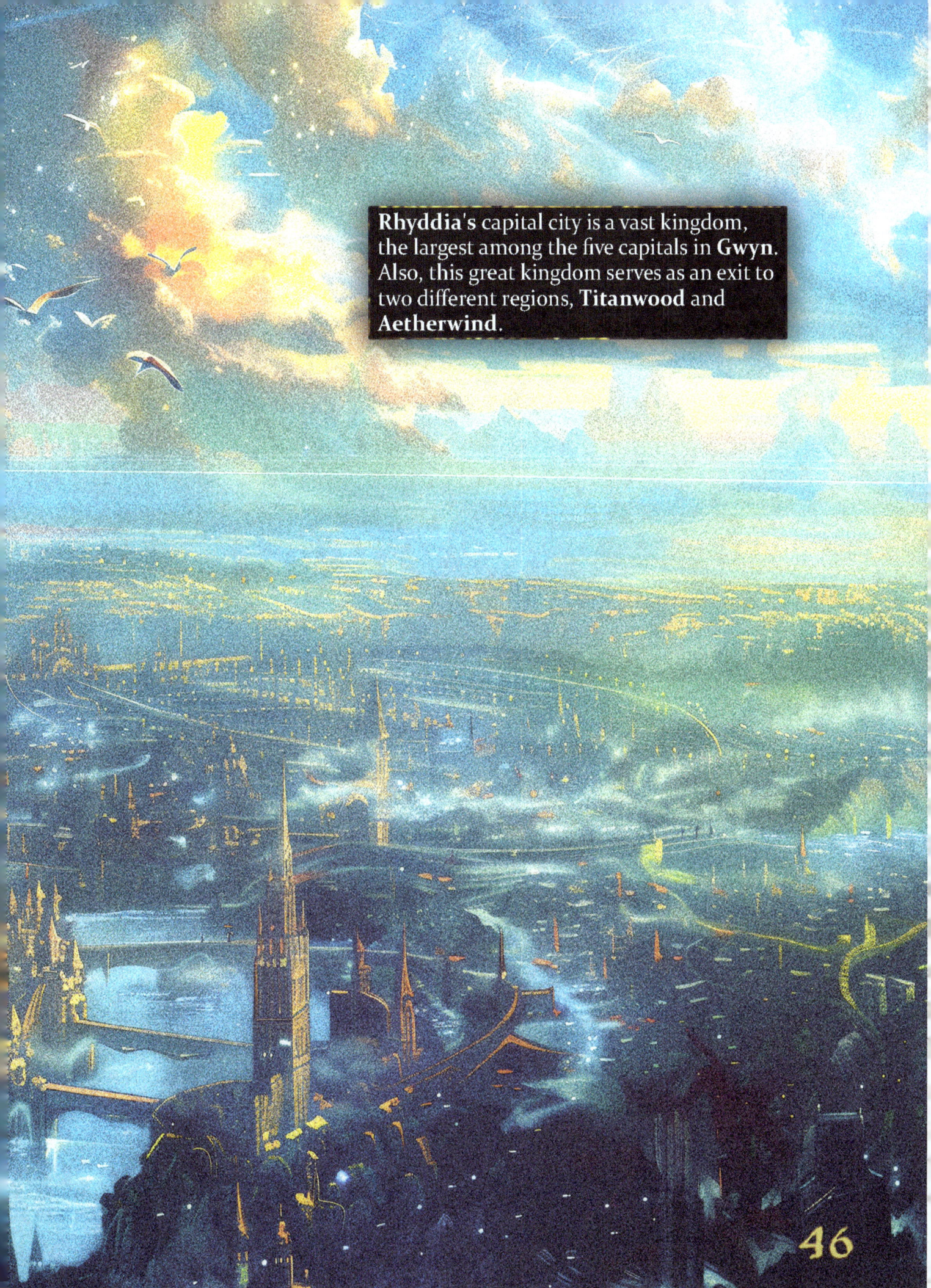

Rhyddia's capital city is a vast kingdom, the largest among the five capitals in **Gwyn**. Also, this great kingdom serves as an exit to two different regions, **Titanwood** and **Aetherwind**.

Map

- Shadowmere
- Mistveil
- Duskenwood
- Mordrakar
- Vantamist
- Tanbryn

Ebonholt

There are unique creatures that only exist here, born during the **Age of Frey**. The northern part of **Ebonholt** has tall mountains and large volcanoes, while the south has flatter terrain with many forests. In this area, nature doesn't turn green; instead, it becomes a faded orange in the summer. During winter, a mystical weather phenomenon causes the country to crystallise like a fungus, forming dark purple crystals from non-living matter. The continent consists of five nations: **Shadowmere**, **Duskenwood**, **Mistveil**, **Vantamist**, and **Tanbryn**, with the capital **Mordrakar** located at the borders of three of these nations. This nation holds a strong alliance with **Bloodmoon Isle**.

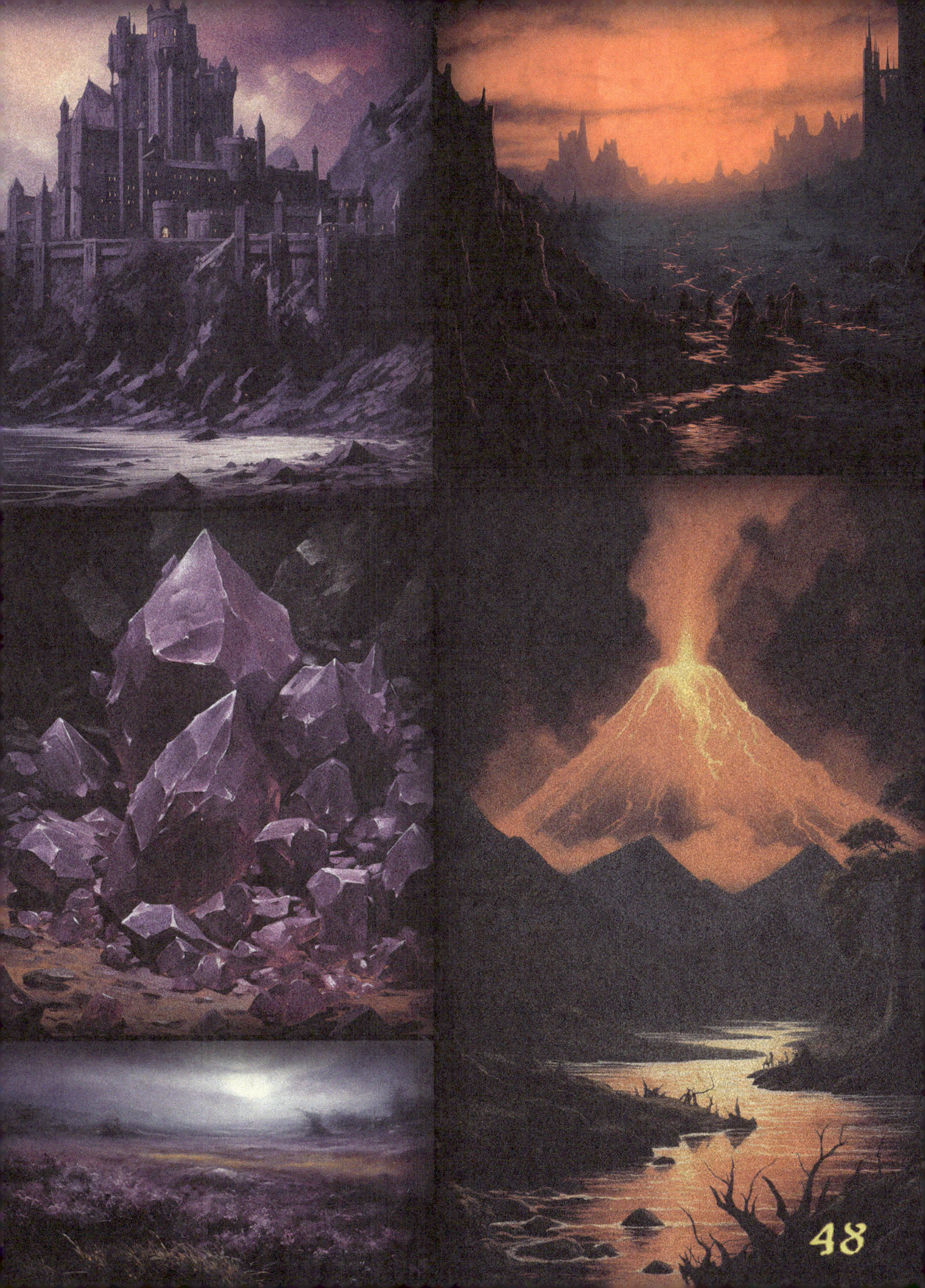

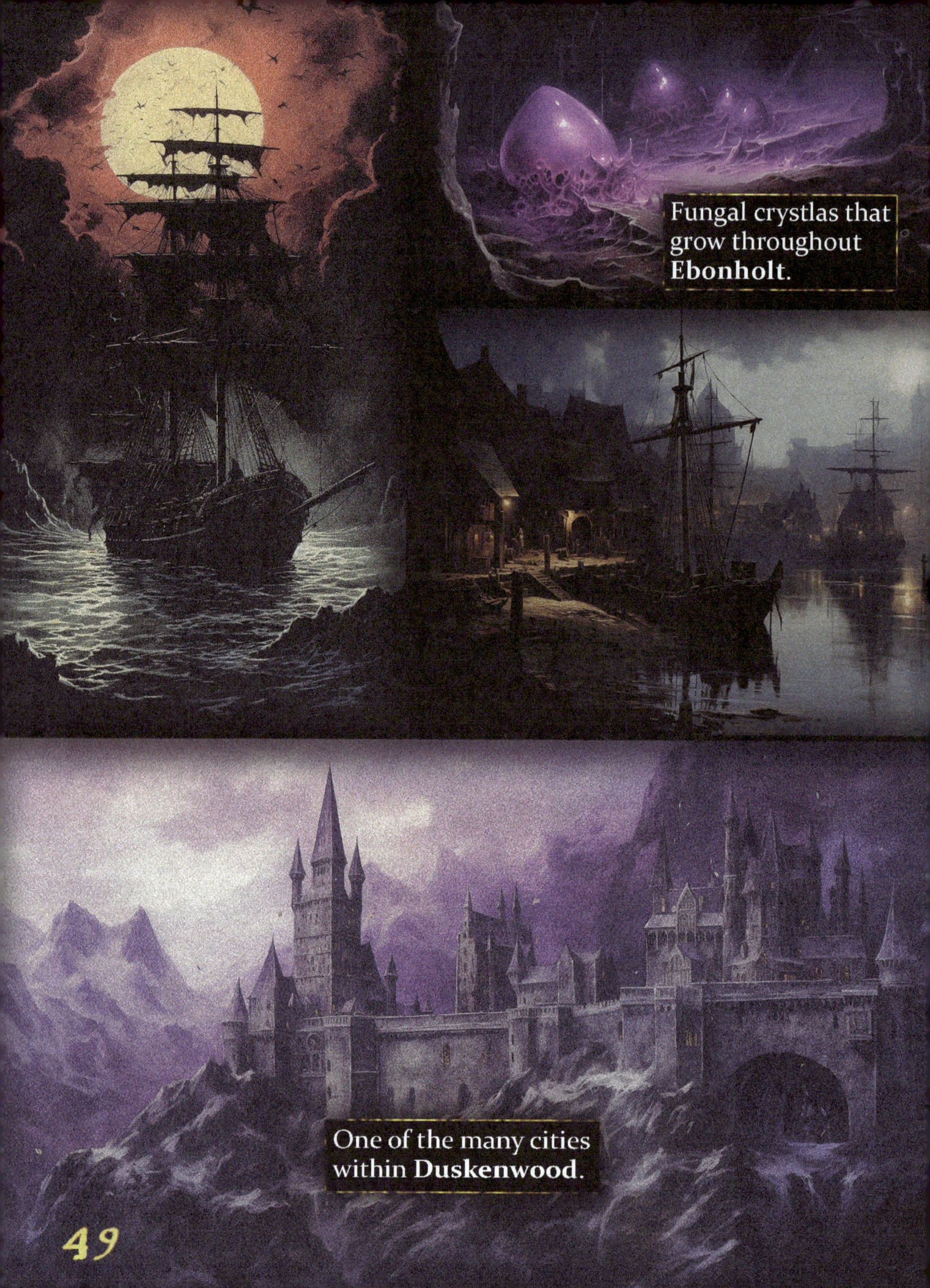

Fungal crystlas that grow throughout **Ebonholt**.

One of the many cities within **Duskenwood**.

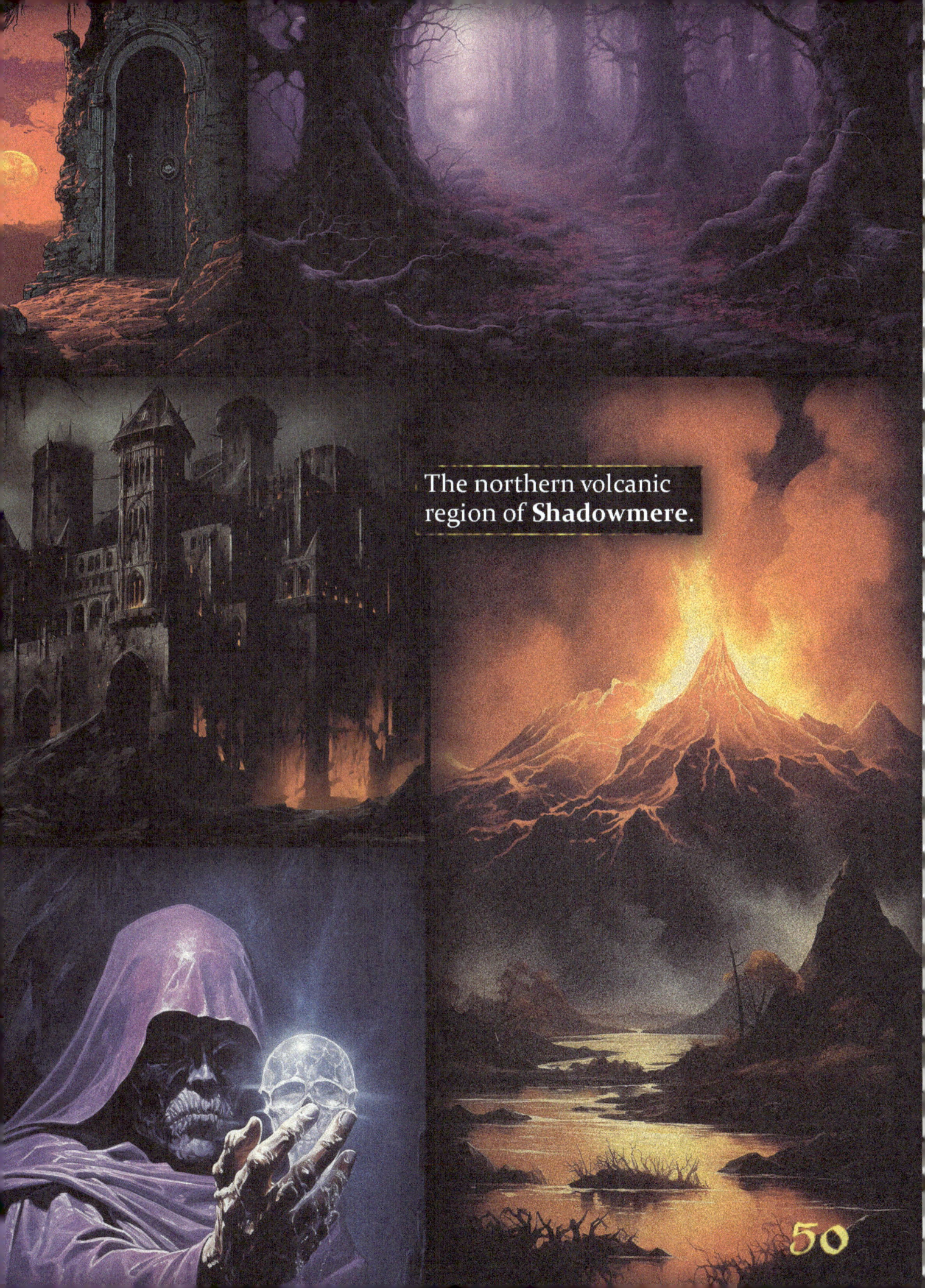

The northern volcanic region of **Shadowmere**.

Mordrakar

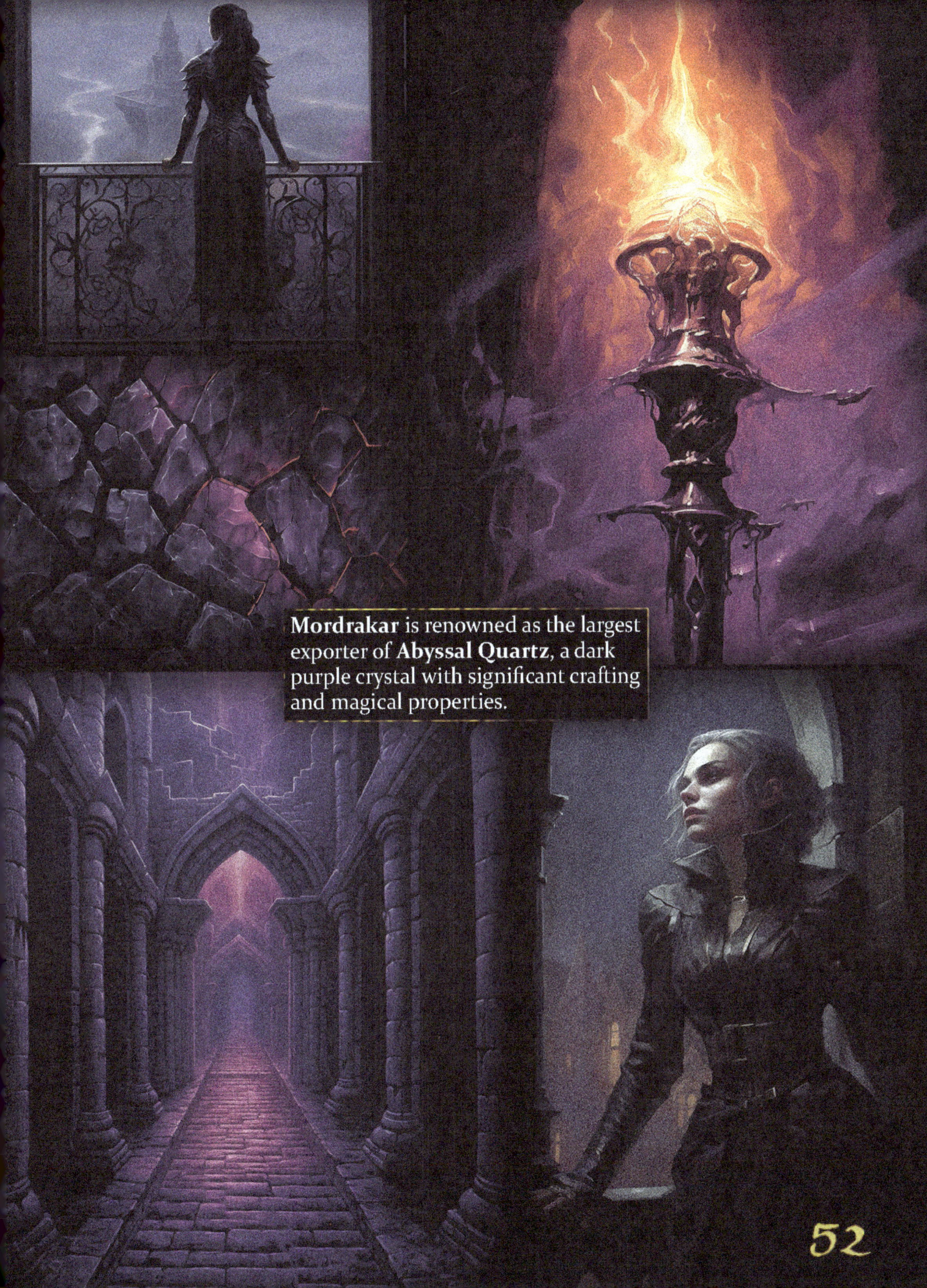

Mordrakar is renowned as the largest exporter of **Abyssal Quartz**, a dark purple crystal with significant crafting and magical properties.

Bloodmoon Isle

Bloodmoon Isle is a big island with a crescent moon shape. The northern part is a flat lowland covered in magma rock and limestone. As you go south, the land gets higher, leading to vast mountains in **Bloodmoon South**. Some areas of **Bloodmoon Isle** have grass, but it's a faded green in summer and dark grey in winter. These wooded regions are only in the northwest. On the southwest coast of **Crimson Rifts**, there's a huge underground cavern with a crystal blue lake containing a godly essence called **Maelgors Peace**. The capital city, **Bloodveil**, is ruled by **King Morvus Blackthorn**.

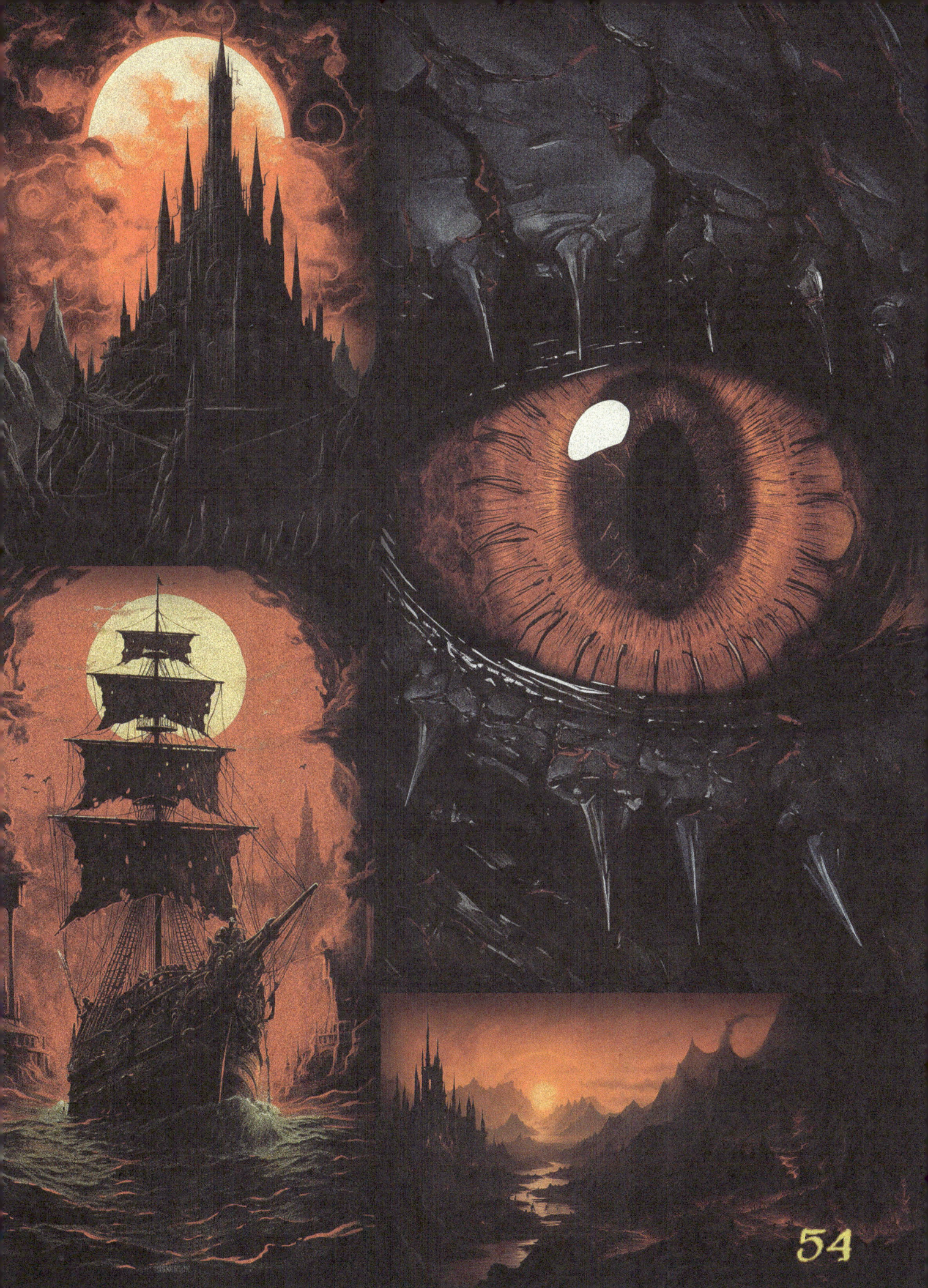

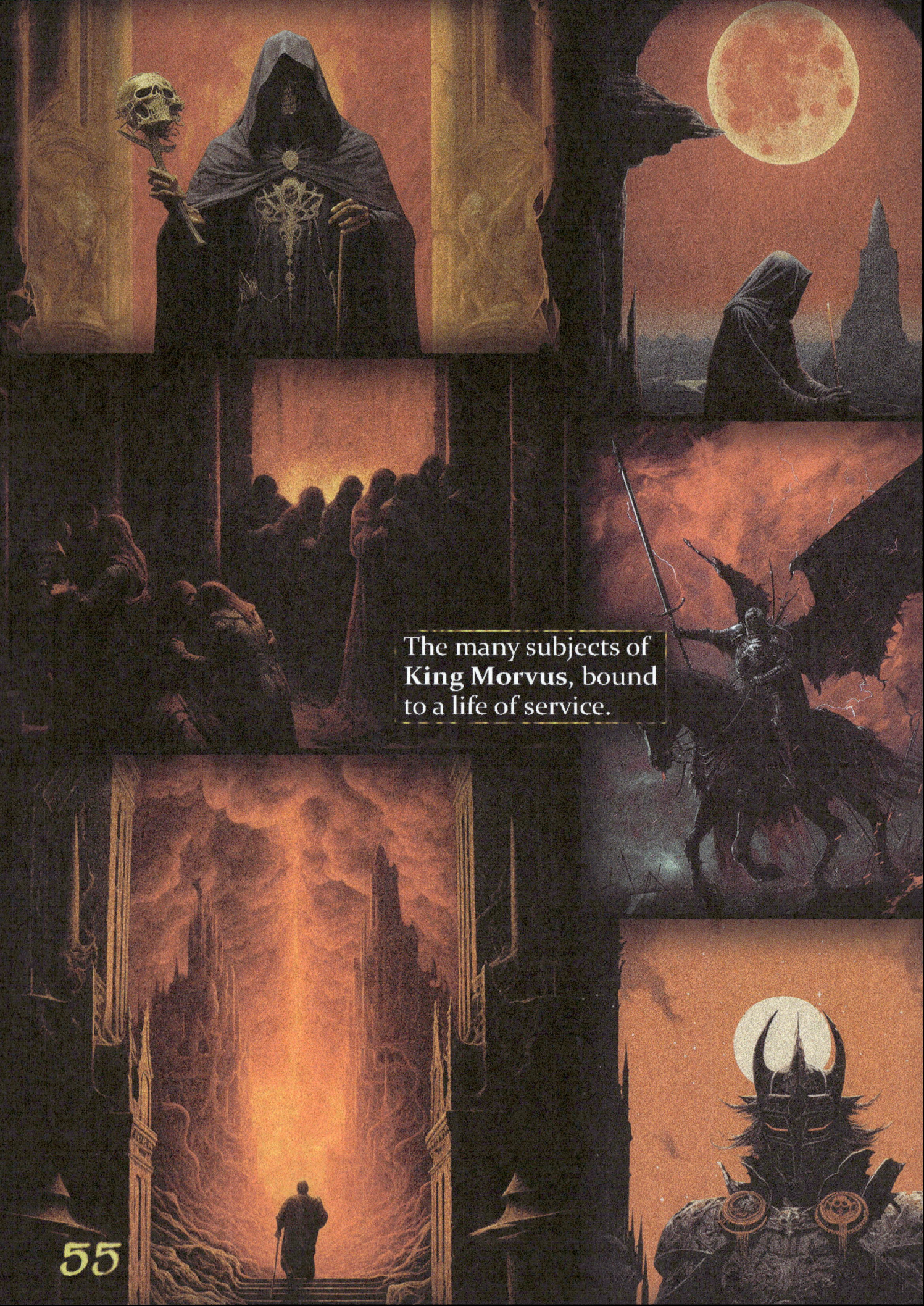

The many subjects of **King Morvus**, bound to a life of service.

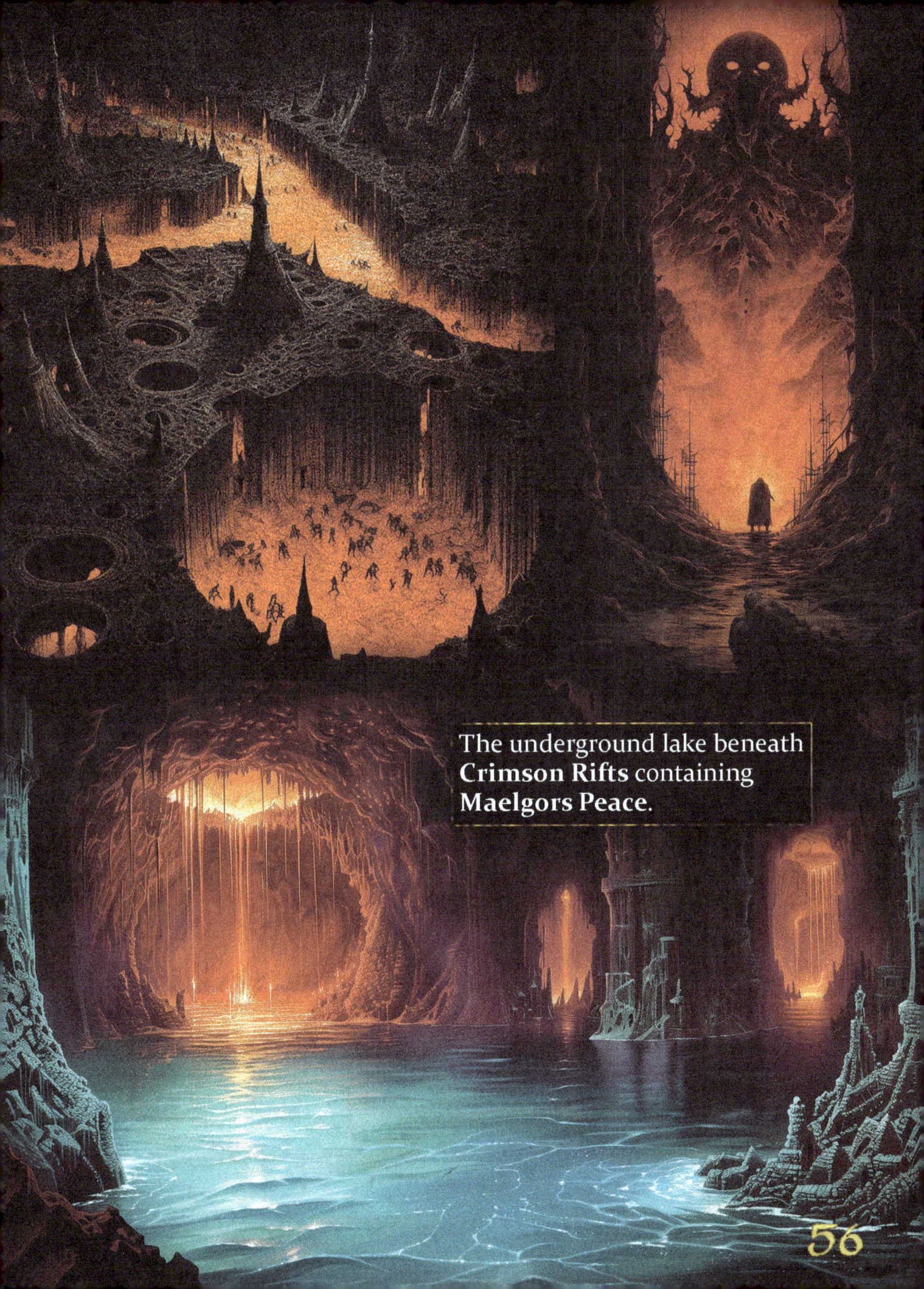

The underground lake beneath **Crimson Rifts** containing **Maelgors Peace**.

Bloodveil

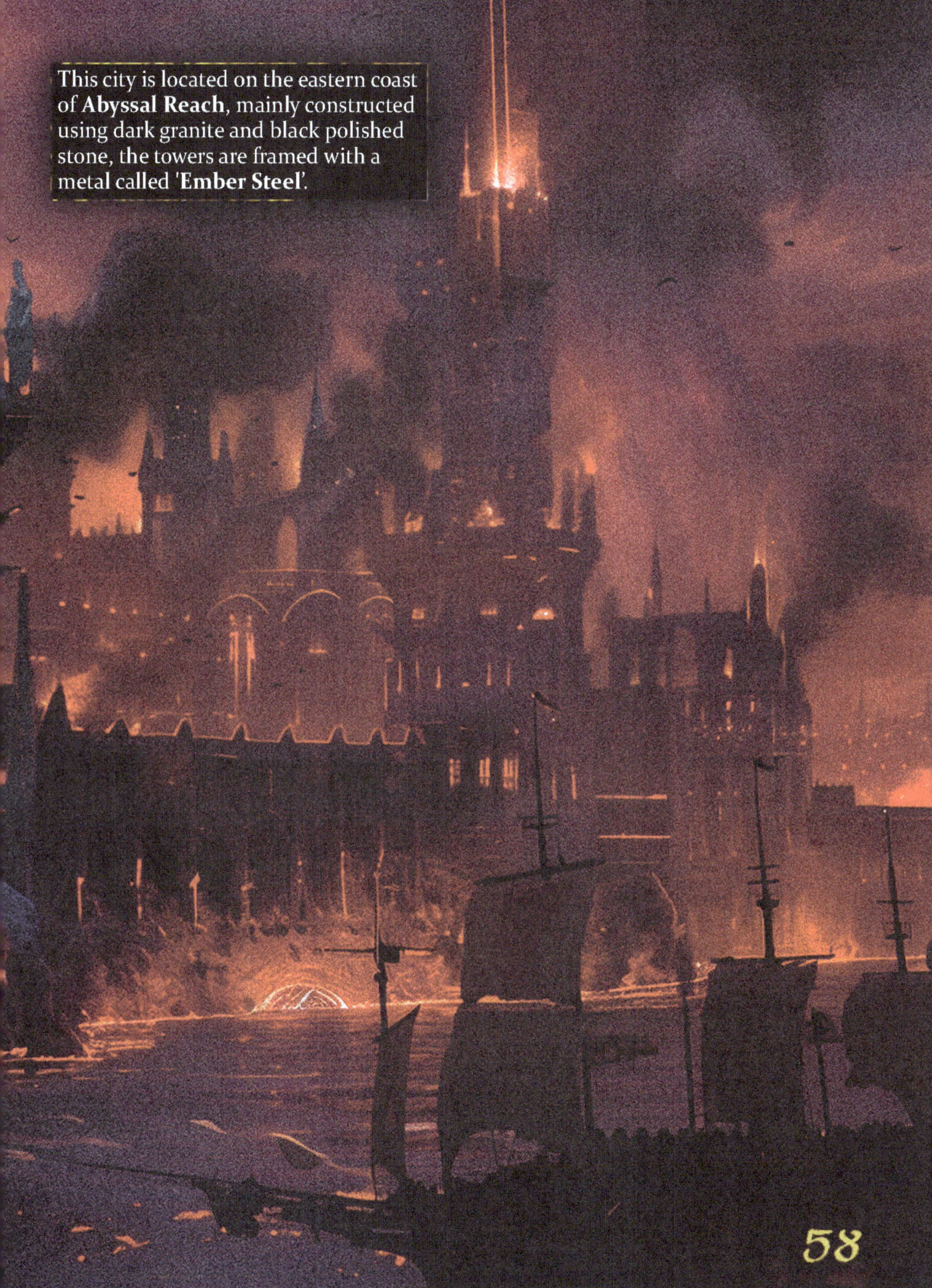

This city is located on the eastern coast of **Abyssal Reach**, mainly constructed using dark granite and black polished stone, the towers are framed with a metal called '**Ember Steel**'.

Evergreen Jungle

The **Evergreen Jungle** is a region not controlled by any nation in **Gwyn**; the area is too uninhabitable due to the mass amounts of wildlife lurking in the jungle. There is a significant amount of potent magical essence in the soil of this jungle, which many travellers often attempt to obtain, though this proves to be quite challenging. Natural inhabitants of the jungle exist; however, they are far removed from the conflicts of the outside world. Only a few are allowed to traverse through the **Evergreen Jungle**, but there are some known routes. It is known as the '**Lungs of Gwyn**'.

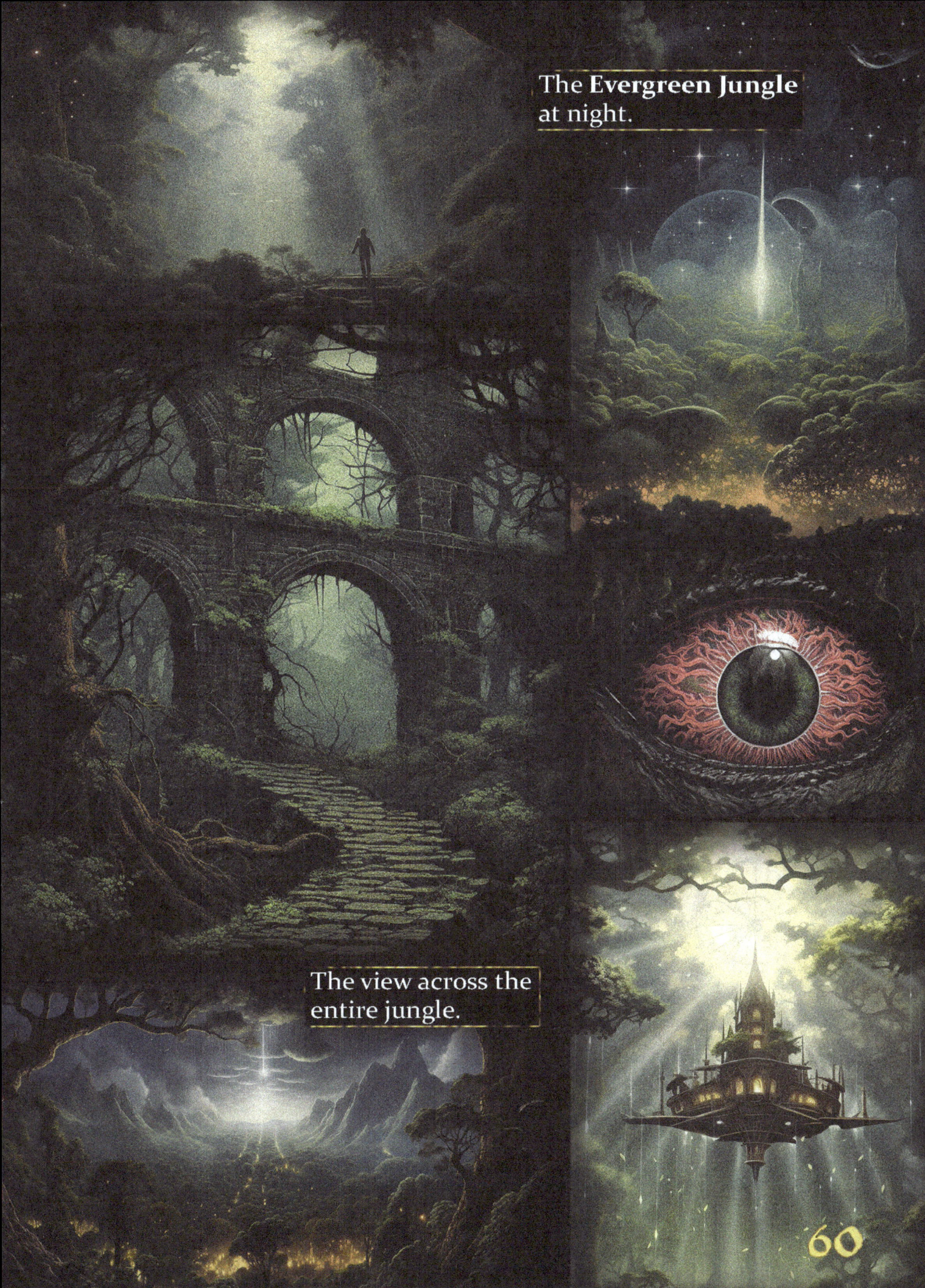

The **Evergreen Jungle** at night.

The view across the entire jungle.

Beasts & Creatures

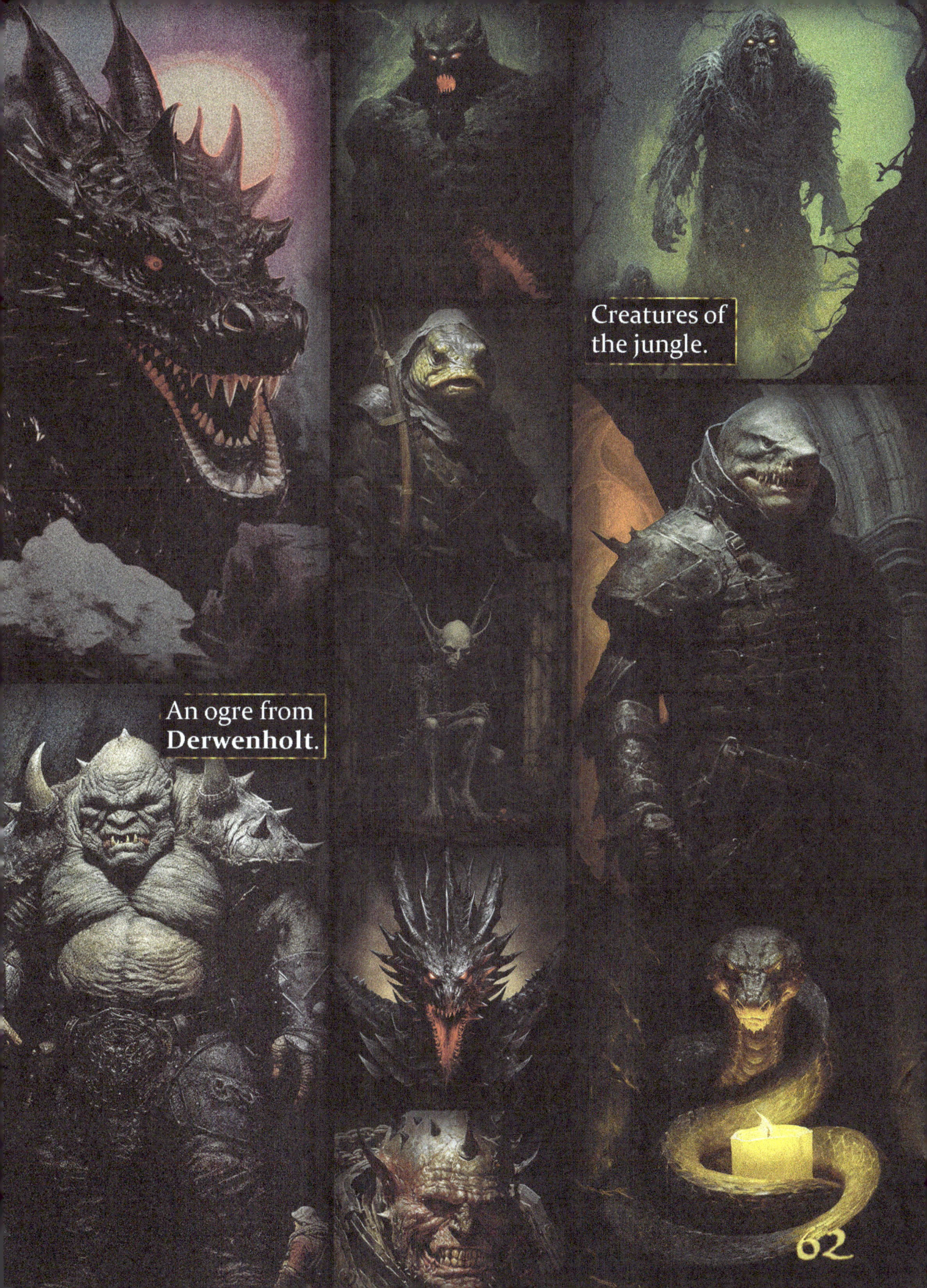

Creatures of the jungle.

An ogre from **Derwenholt**.

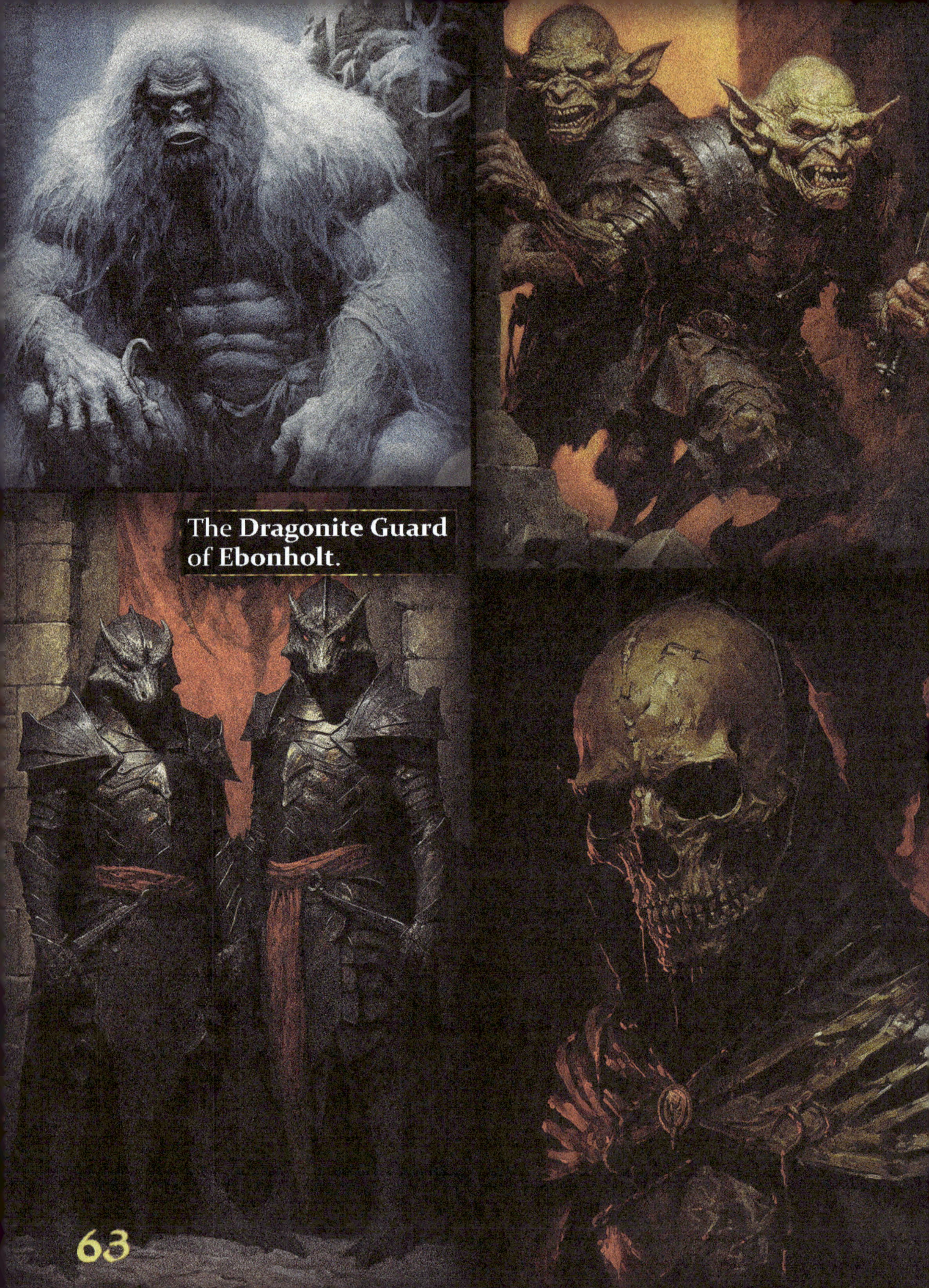

The **Dragonite Guard** of **Ebonholt**.

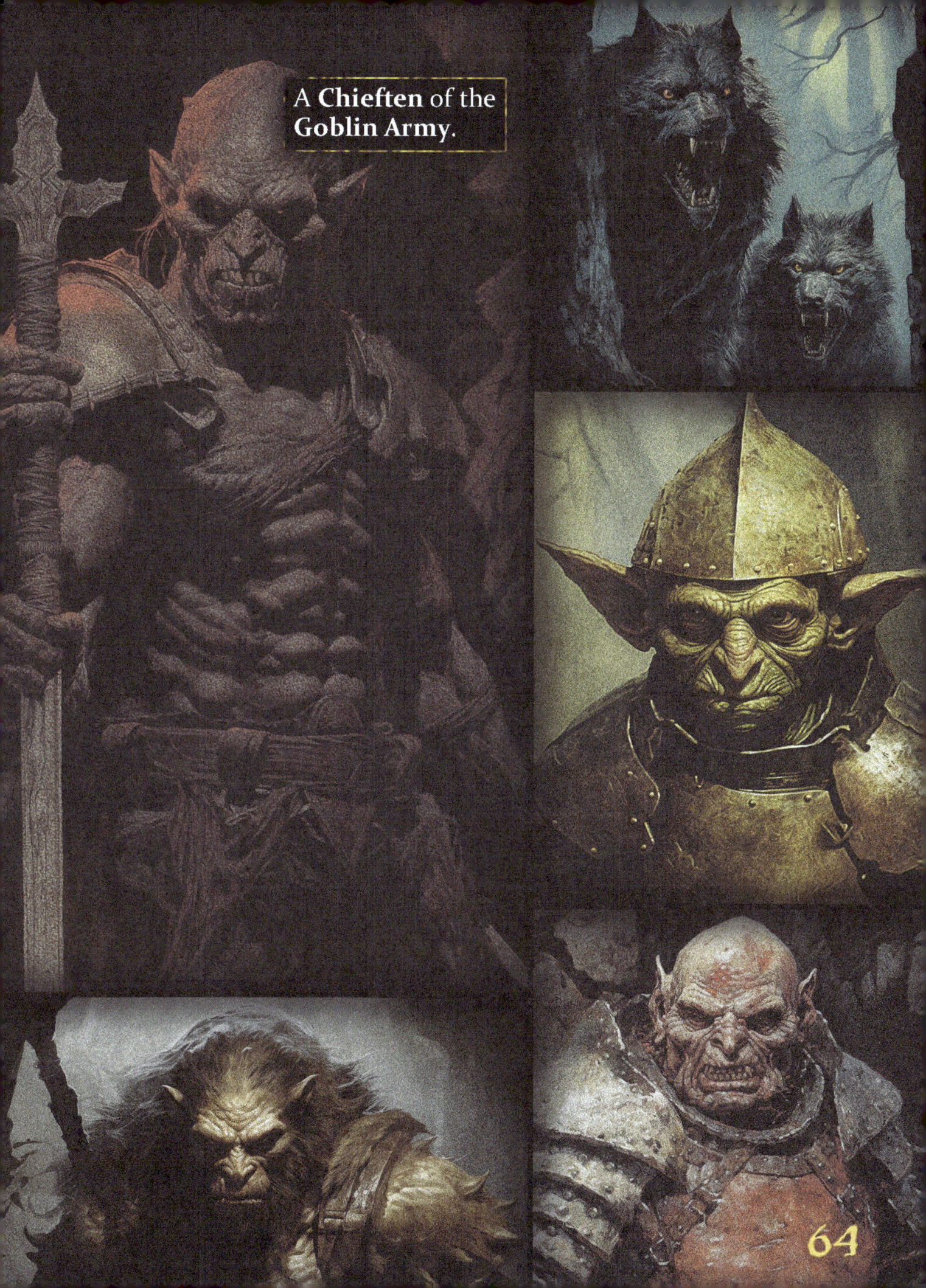

A **Chieften** of the **Goblin Army.**

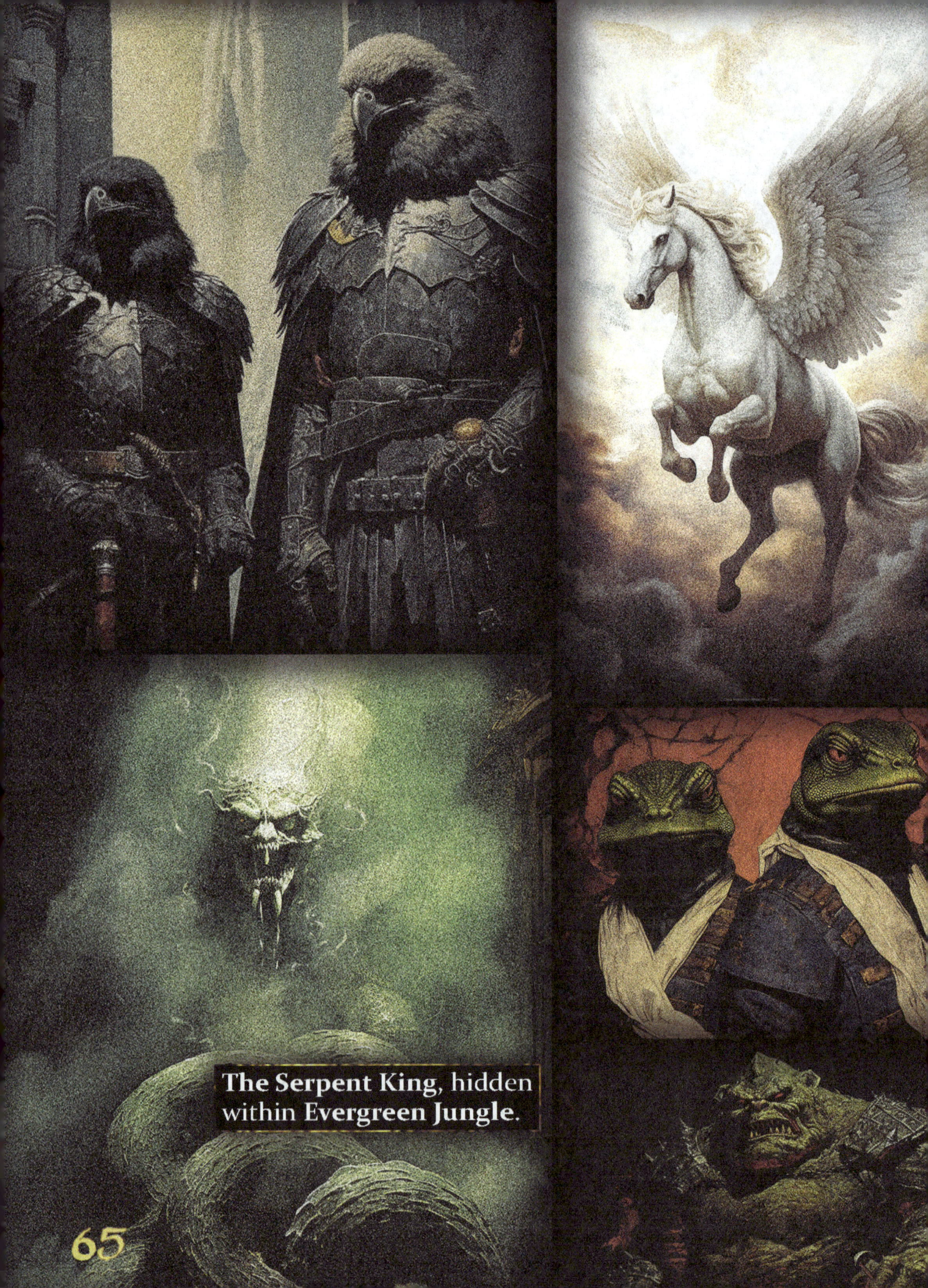

The Serpent King, hidden within Evergreen Jungle.

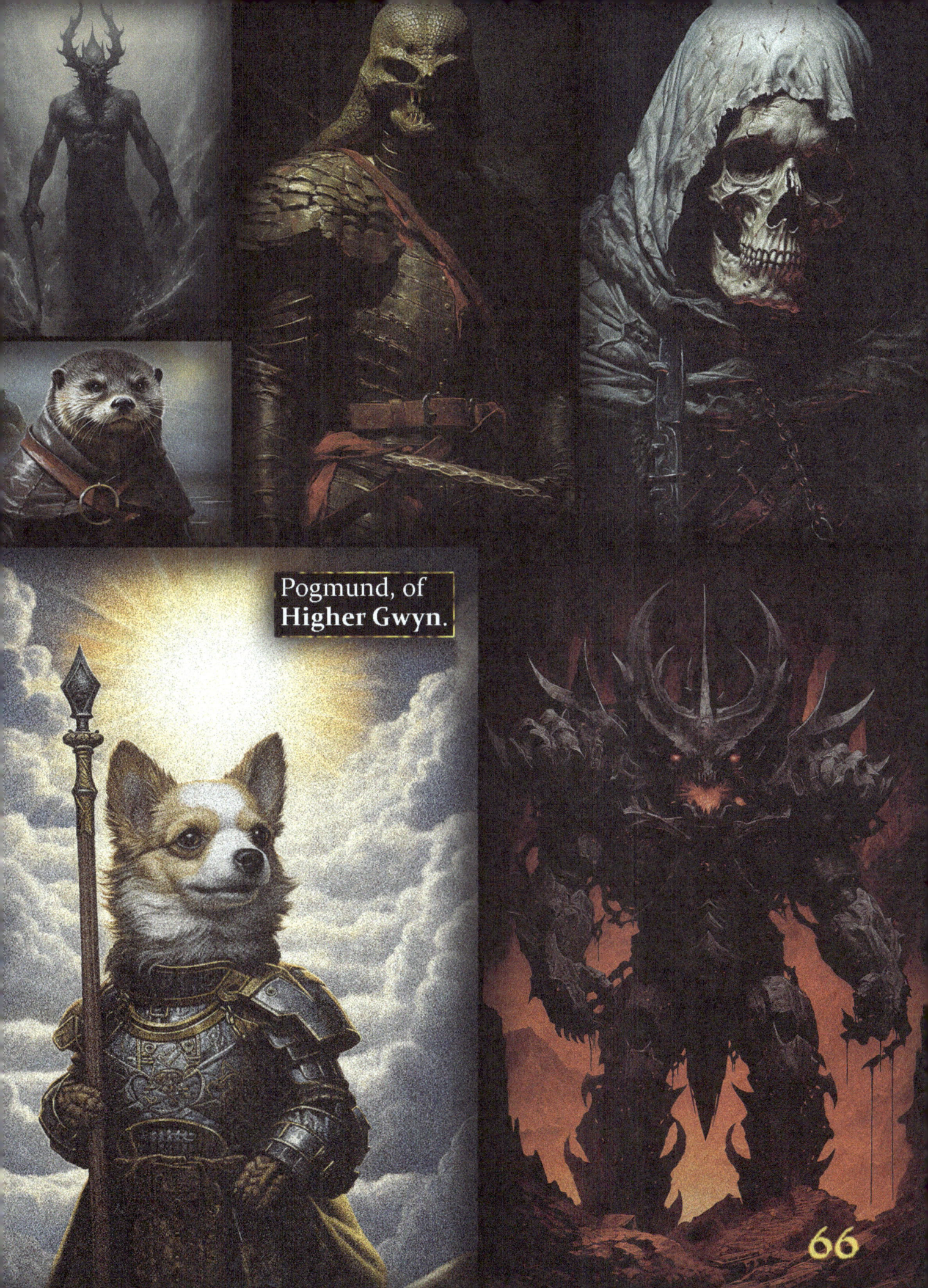

Pogmund, of **Higher Gwyn.**

Elemental Golems

Elemental Golems have the traits and abilities of the elements they come from. These are large creatures, the smallest of which are 9ft tall. **Elemental Golems** started forming in the **Age of Frey**, after the **God Wars** there was lots of godly essence spread out across the realm, when settled in with nature it created life based on the geographical region. If some live long enough then they evolve into more powerful forms.

Earth Golem
These golems form from the soil in the region of **Tanbryn**.

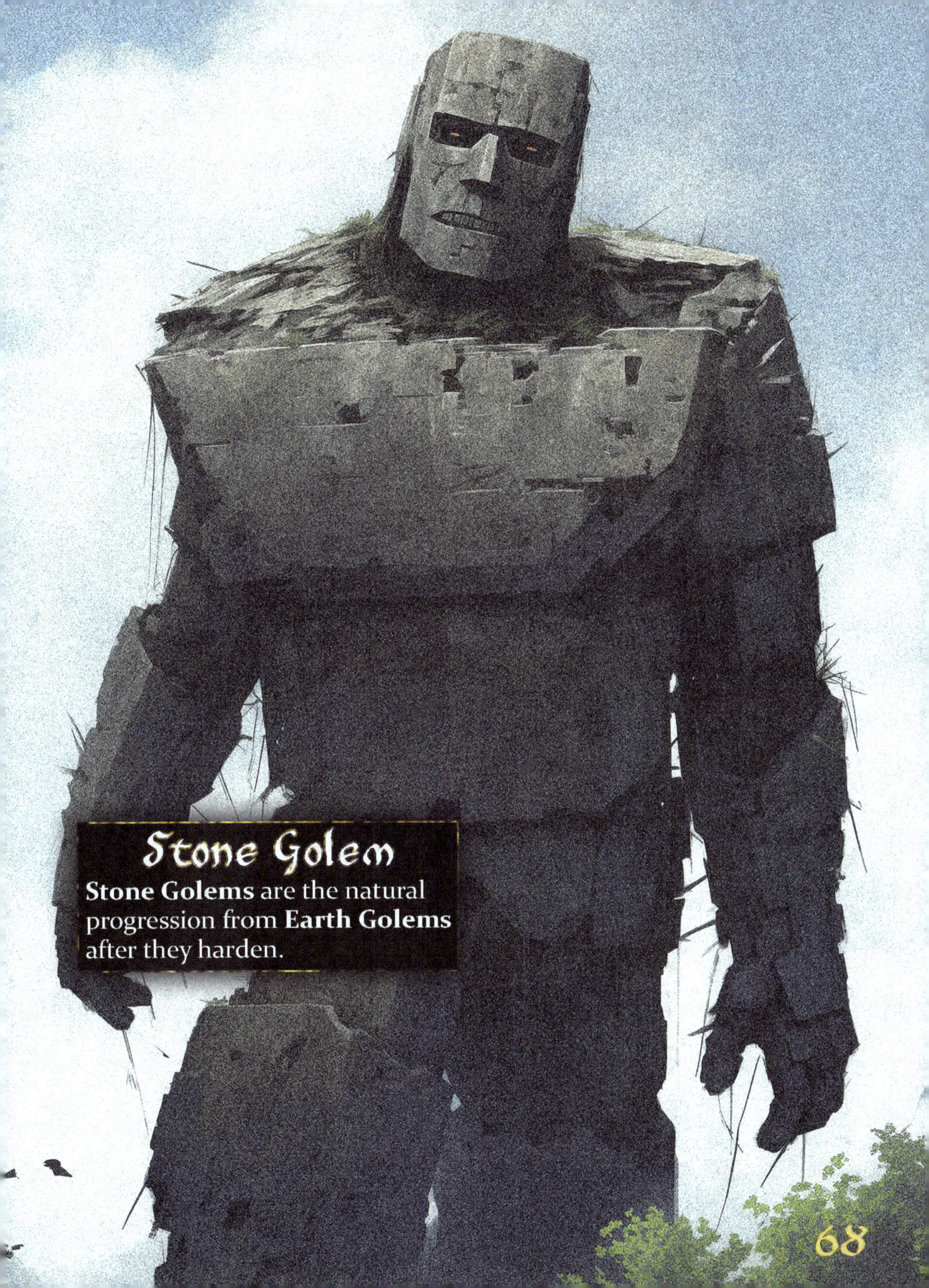

Stone Golem

Stone Golems are the natural progression from **Earth Golems** after they harden.

Wood Golem

Emerging from trees in the region of **Greenbriar**.

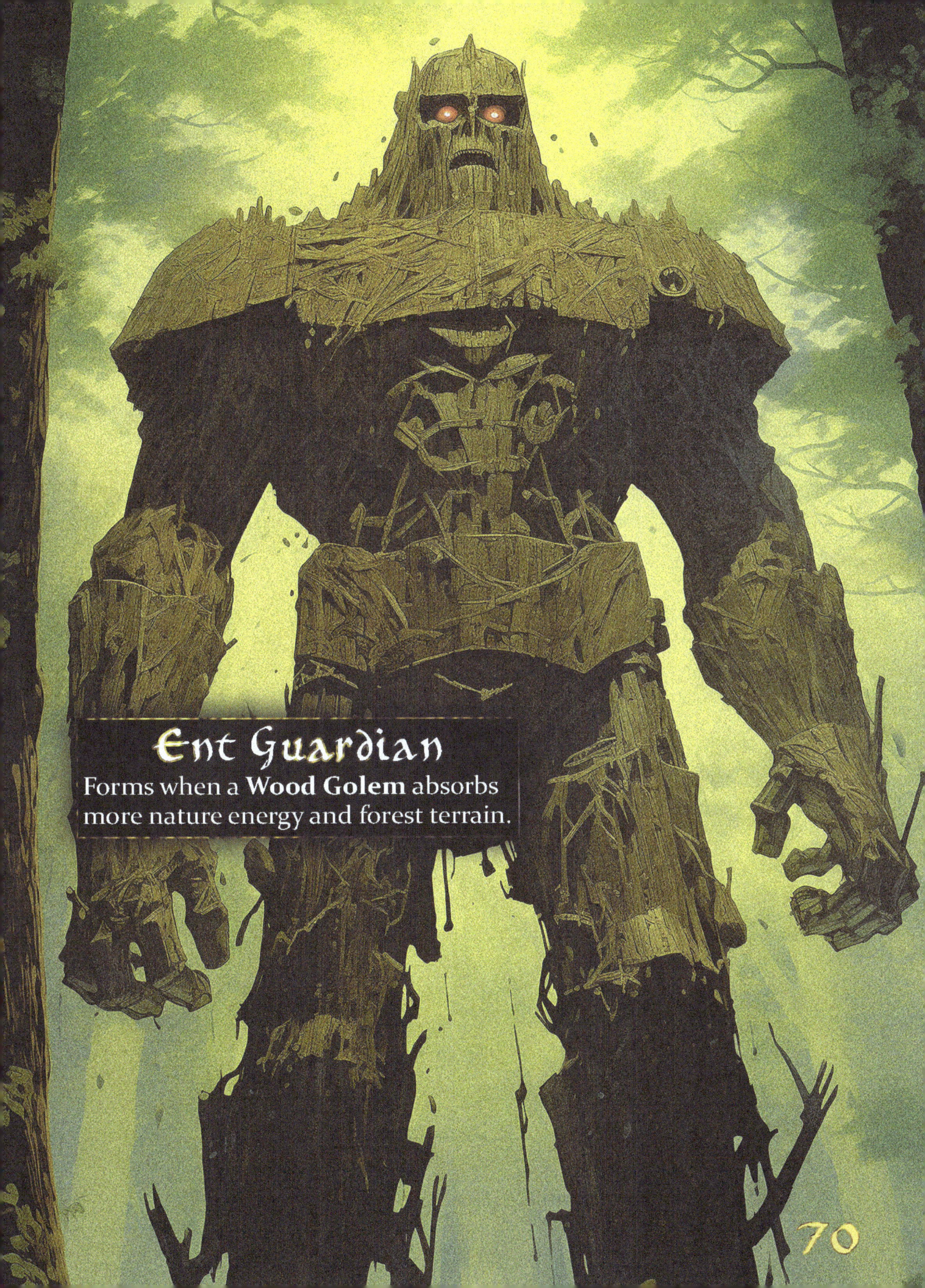

Ent Guardian
Forms when a **Wood Golem** absorbs more nature energy and forest terrain.

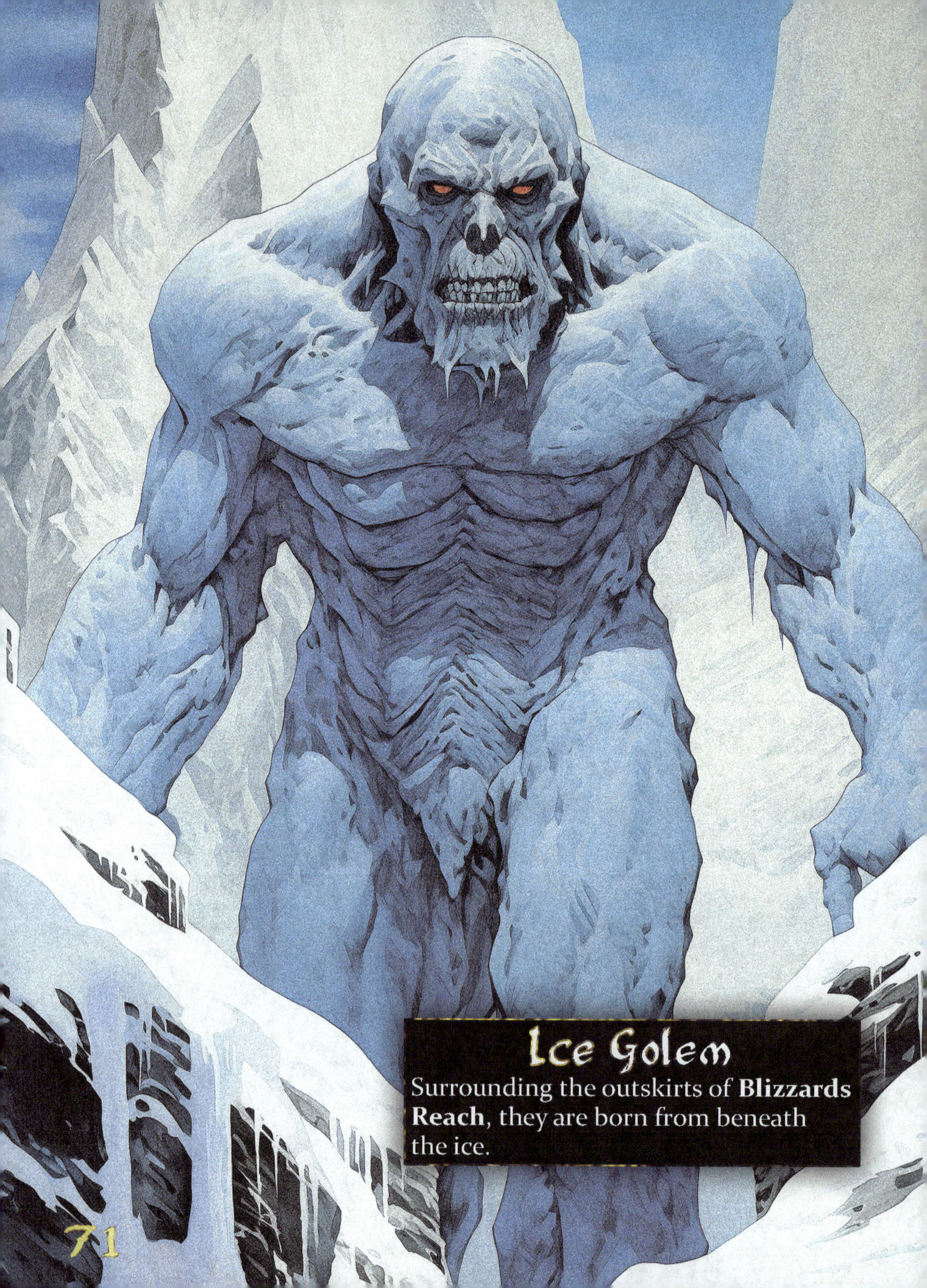

Ice Golem
Surrounding the outskirts of **Blizzards Reach**, they are born from beneath the ice.

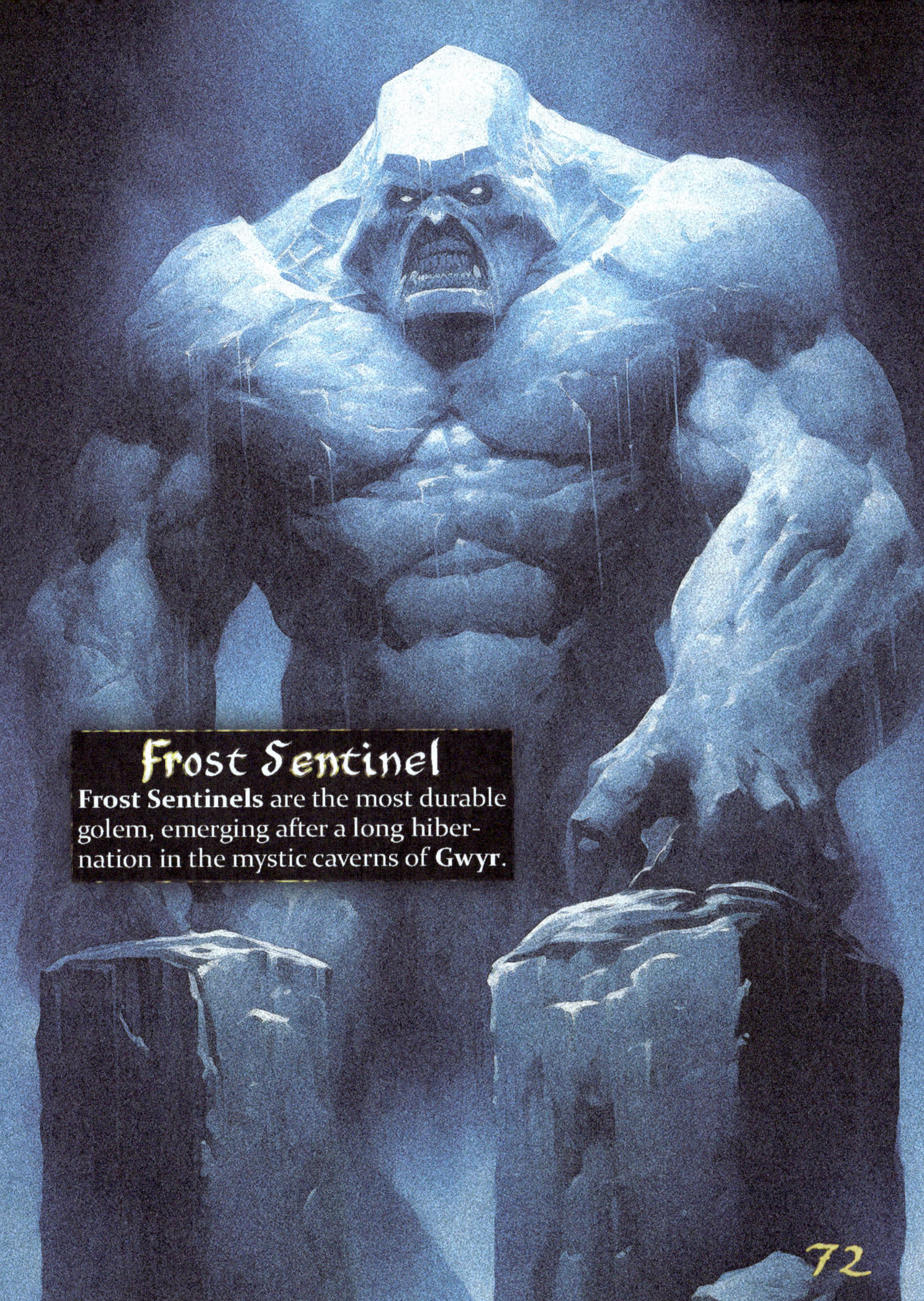

Frost Sentinel

Frost Sentinels are the most durable golem, emerging after a long hibernation in the mystic caverns of **Gwyr**.

Magma Golem

Magma Golems are some of the smallest, forming in the pits of **Bloodmoon South**.

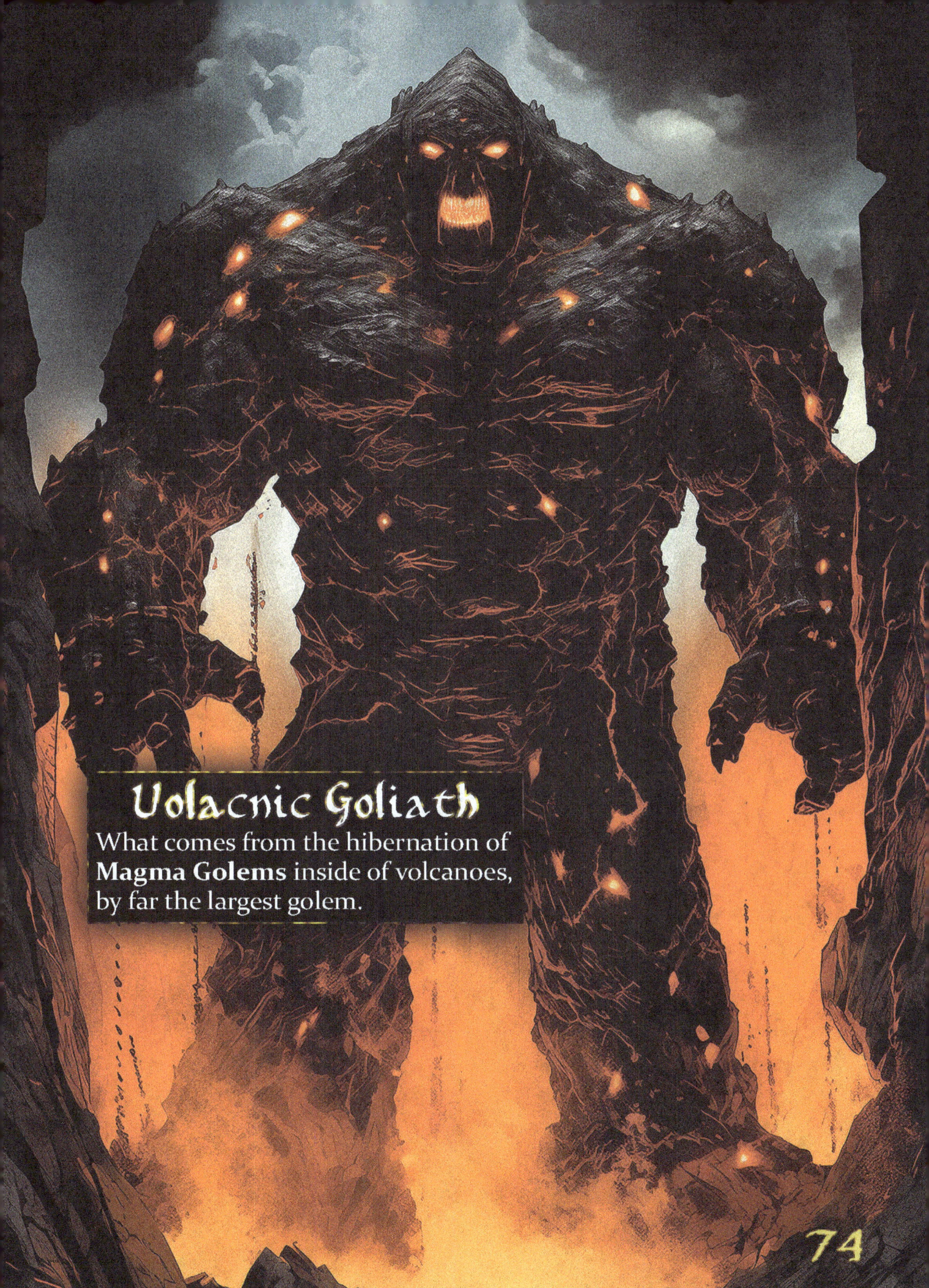

Thunder Golem

Thunder Golems emerge from great storms in the mountains of **Tarannon**.

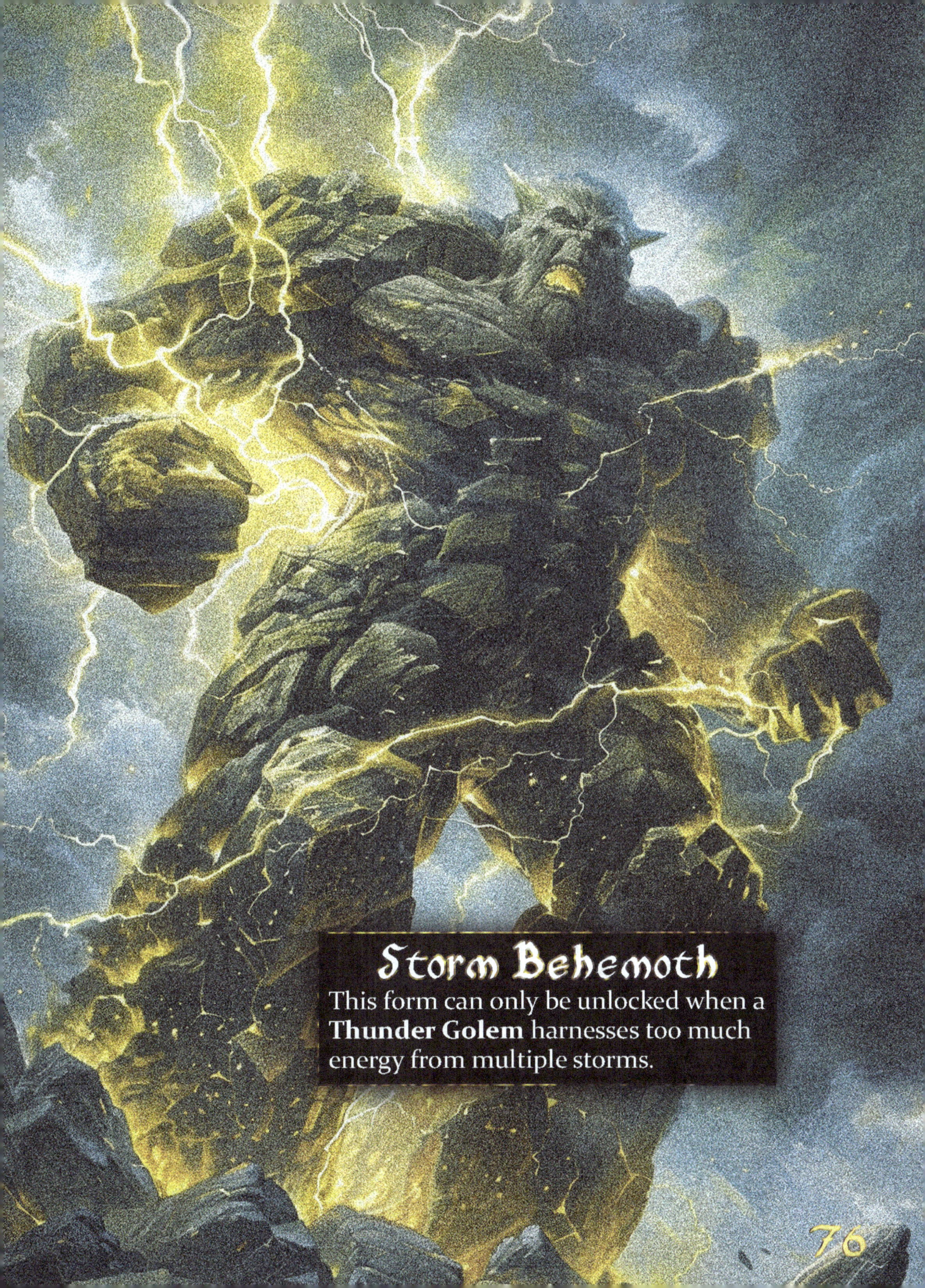

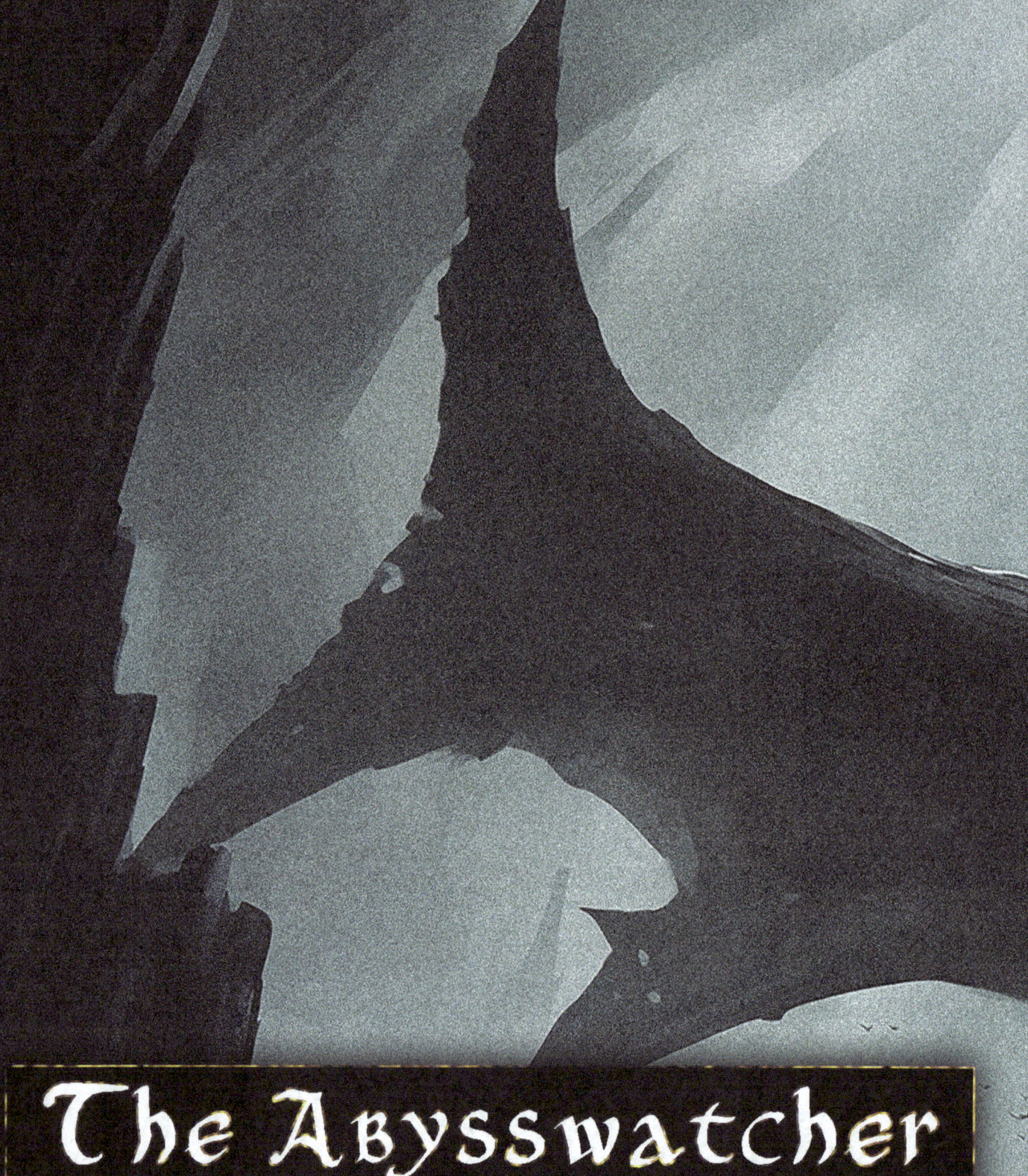

The Abysswatcher

Every year, **The Abysswatcher**, an enormous mystery, appears off the southern coast of **Rhyddia**. Its scaly exterior, a dim mix of black and grey, appears like an enormous whale with bat-like wings. Robust sharp dorsal spikes run along its back, its hide resembling ancient stone. This isolated wanderer's true nature is hidden in silence, it is thought to be the most terrifying force in the entire realm.

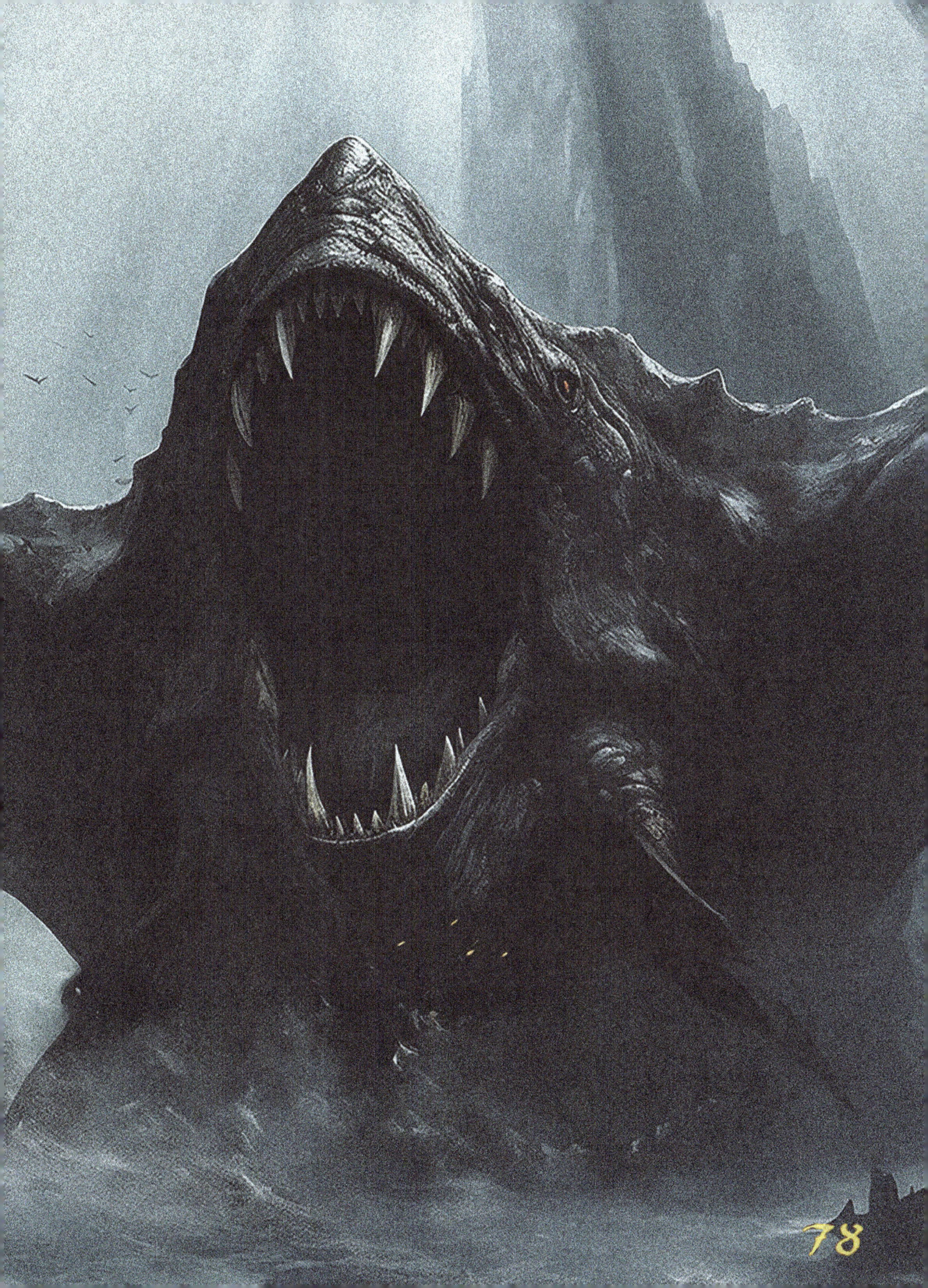

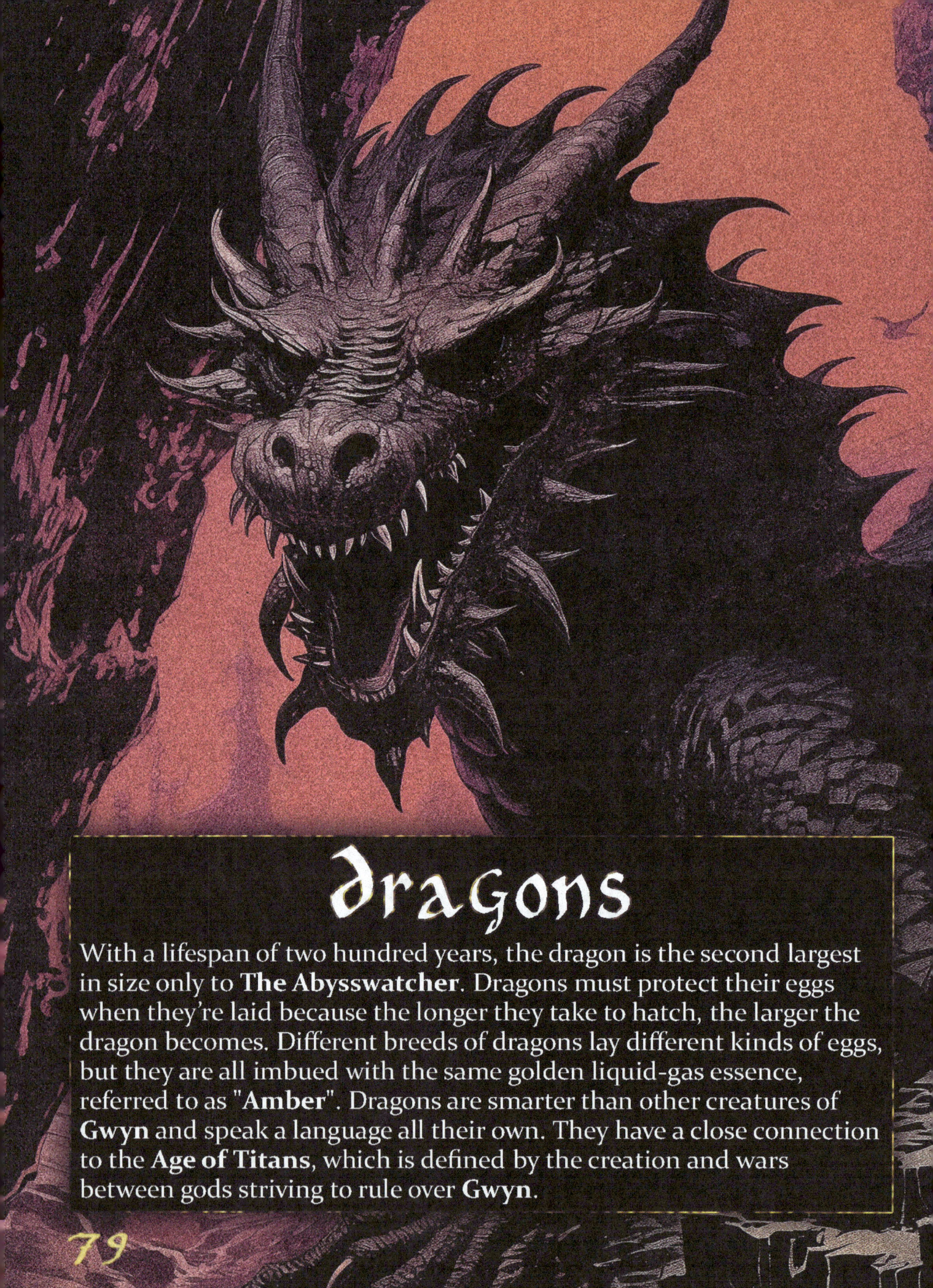

dragons

With a lifespan of two hundred years, the dragon is the second largest in size only to **The Abysswatcher**. Dragons must protect their eggs when they're laid because the longer they take to hatch, the larger the dragon becomes. Different breeds of dragons lay different kinds of eggs, but they are all imbued with the same golden liquid-gas essence, referred to as "**Amber**". Dragons are smarter than other creatures of **Gwyn** and speak a language all their own. They have a close connection to the **Age of Titans**, which is defined by the creation and wars between gods striving to rule over **Gwyn**.

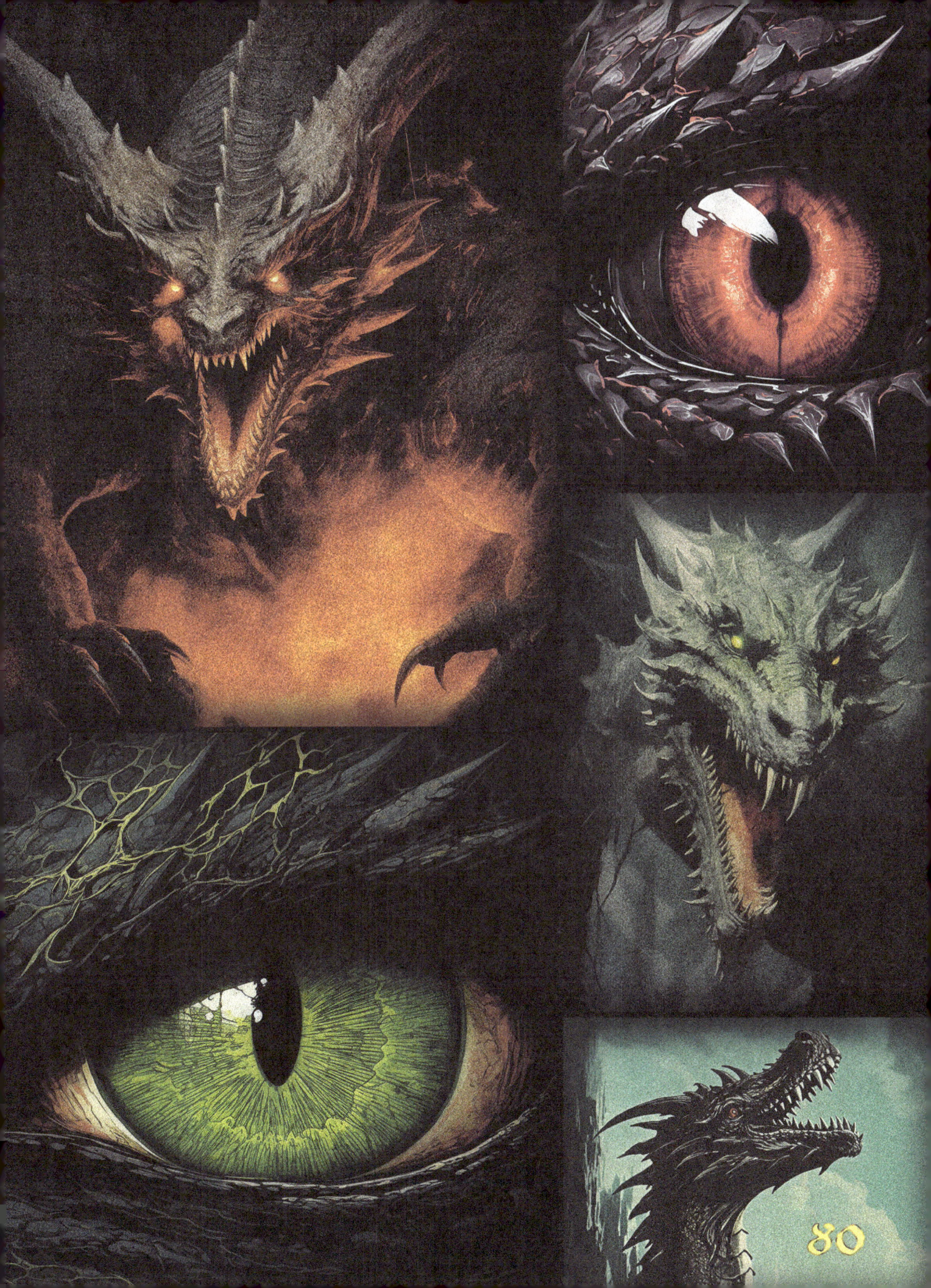

Amber

Amber is a magical, golden, liquid-gas essence that can be captured from dragons. It can be infused in different ways; weapons, armour, spells, potions, summoning, structures, and other specific crafting. It can be transformed into **Amber Mist** as a gas or **Eternal Amber** as a stone by keeping it still for around three days, each form granting different effects. It remains in a liquid or gaseous state in cold environments but solidifies faster in warm ones.

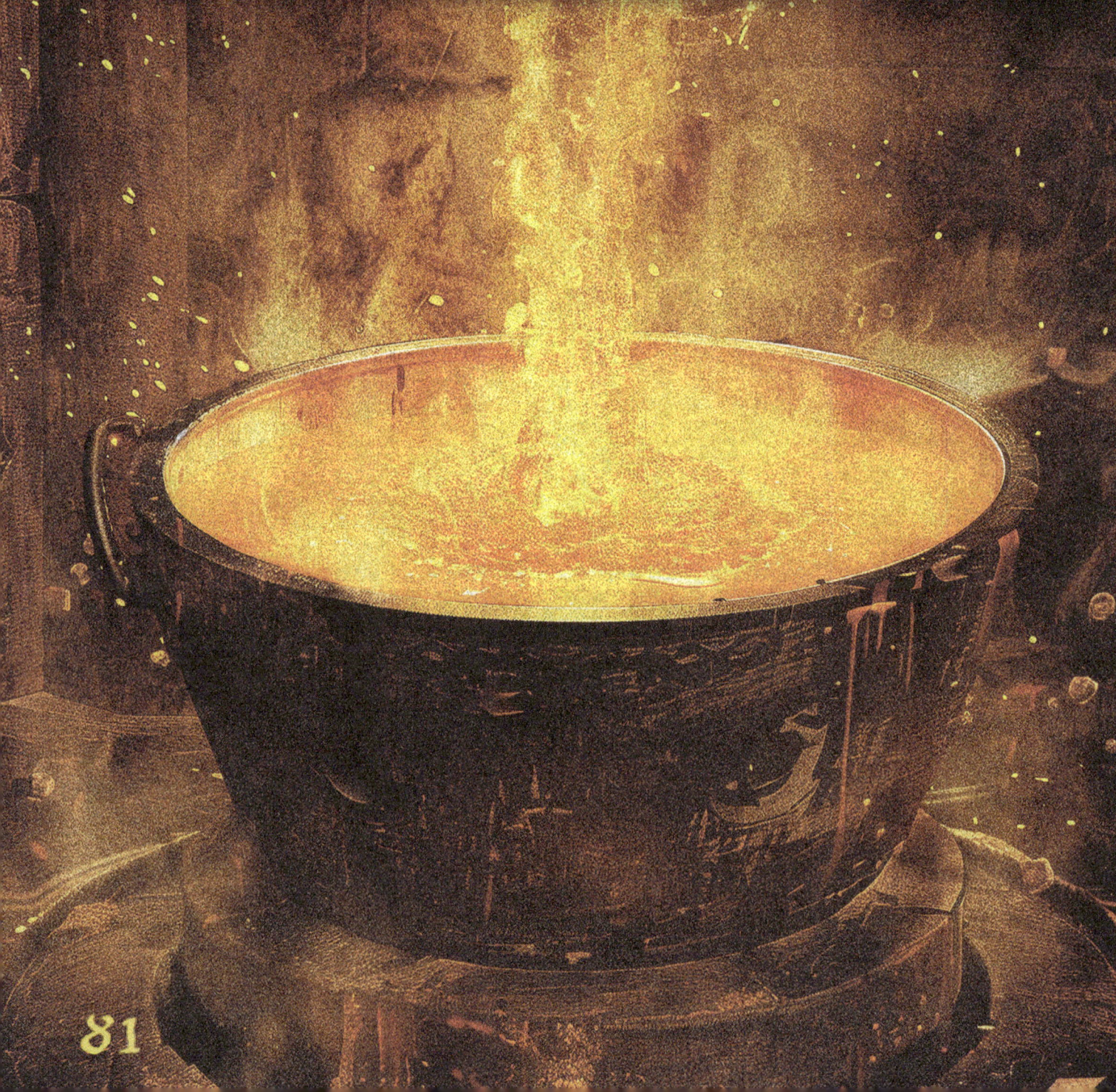

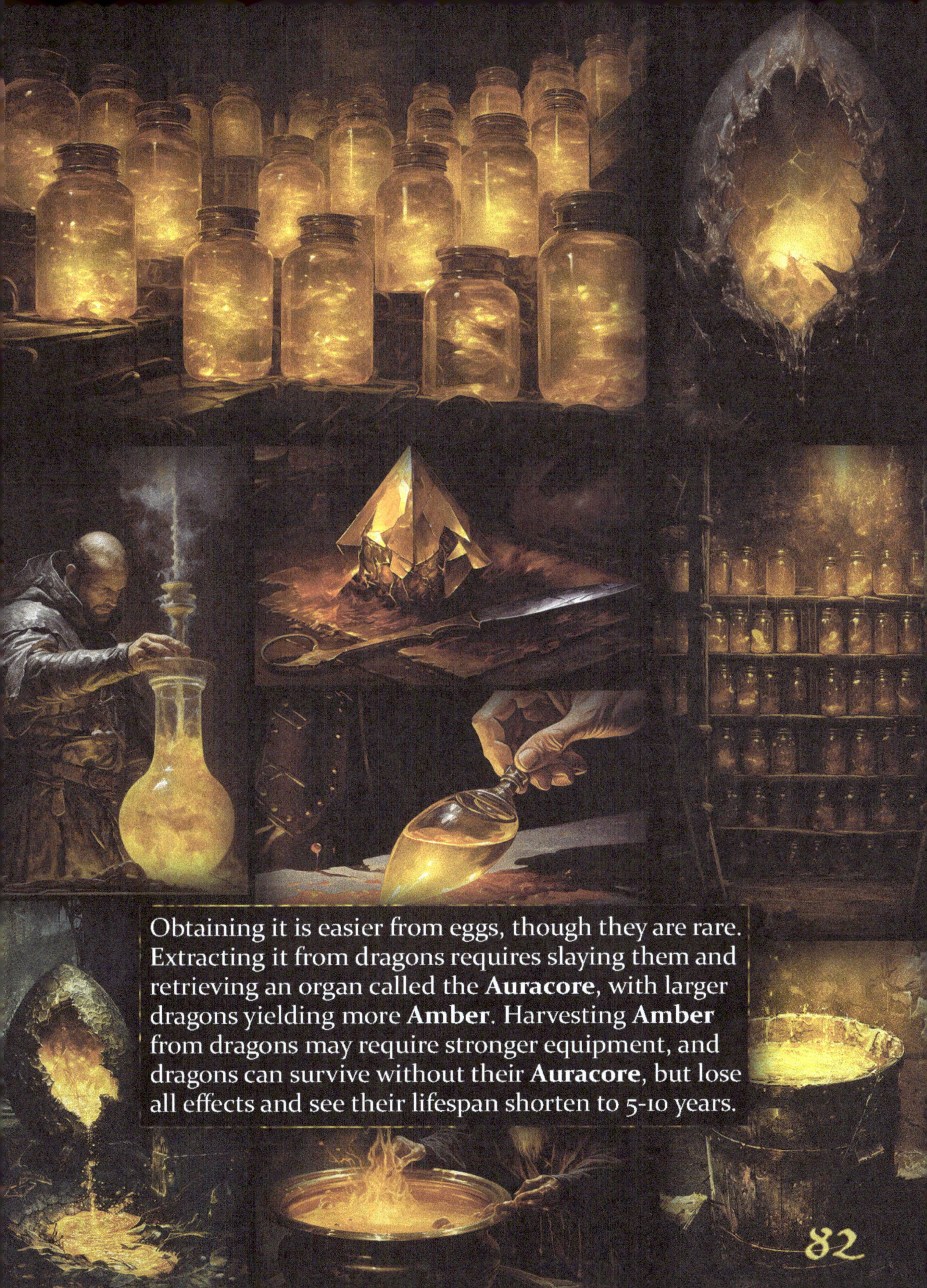

Obtaining it is easier from eggs, though they are rare. Extracting it from dragons requires slaying them and retrieving an organ called the **Auracore**, with larger dragons yielding more **Amber**. Harvesting **Amber** from dragons may require stronger equipment, and dragons can survive without their **Auracore**, but lose all effects and see their lifespan shorten to 5-10 years.

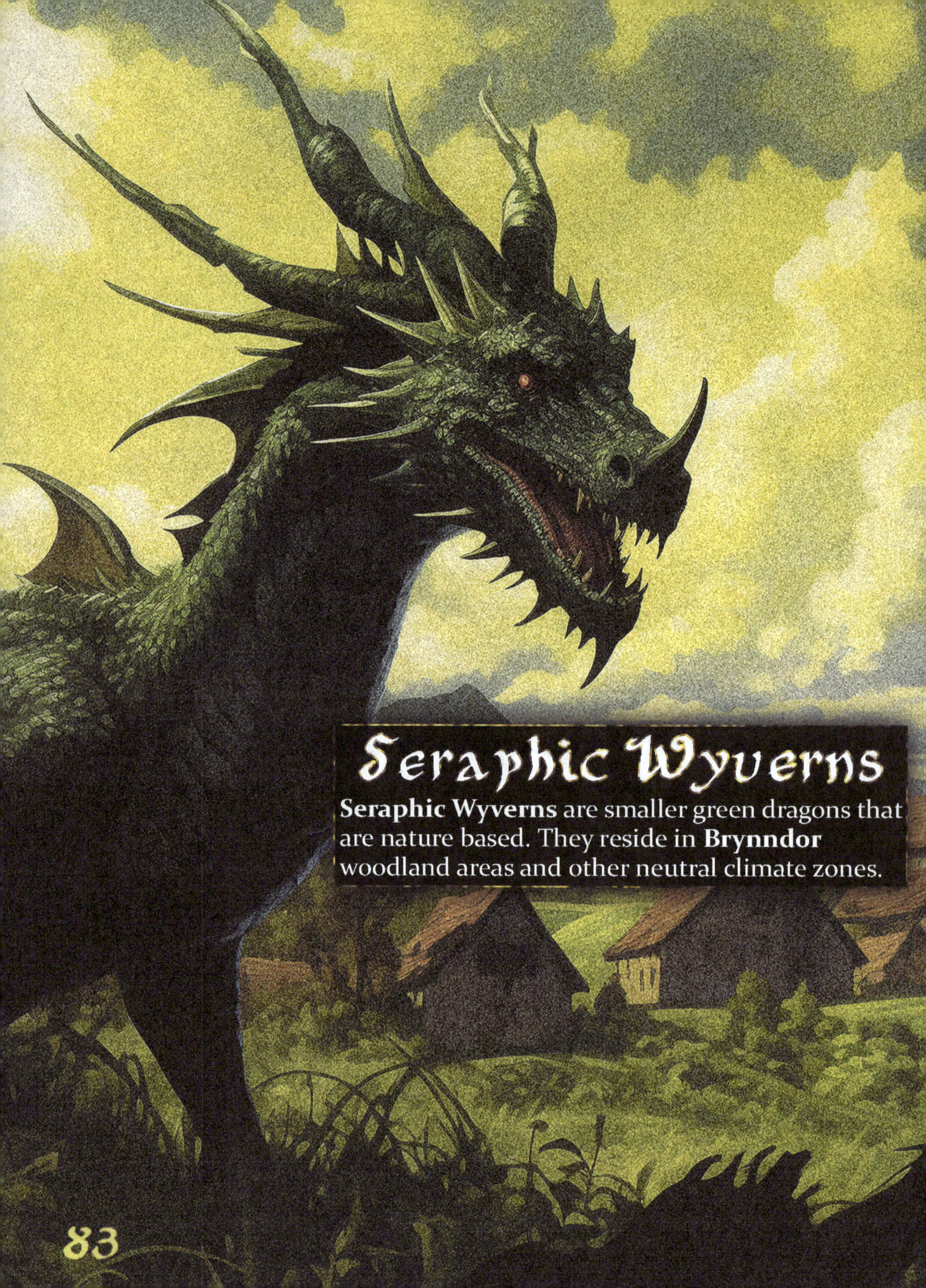

Seraphic Wyverns

Seraphic Wyverns are smaller green dragons that are nature based. They reside in **Brynndor** woodland areas and other neutral climate zones.

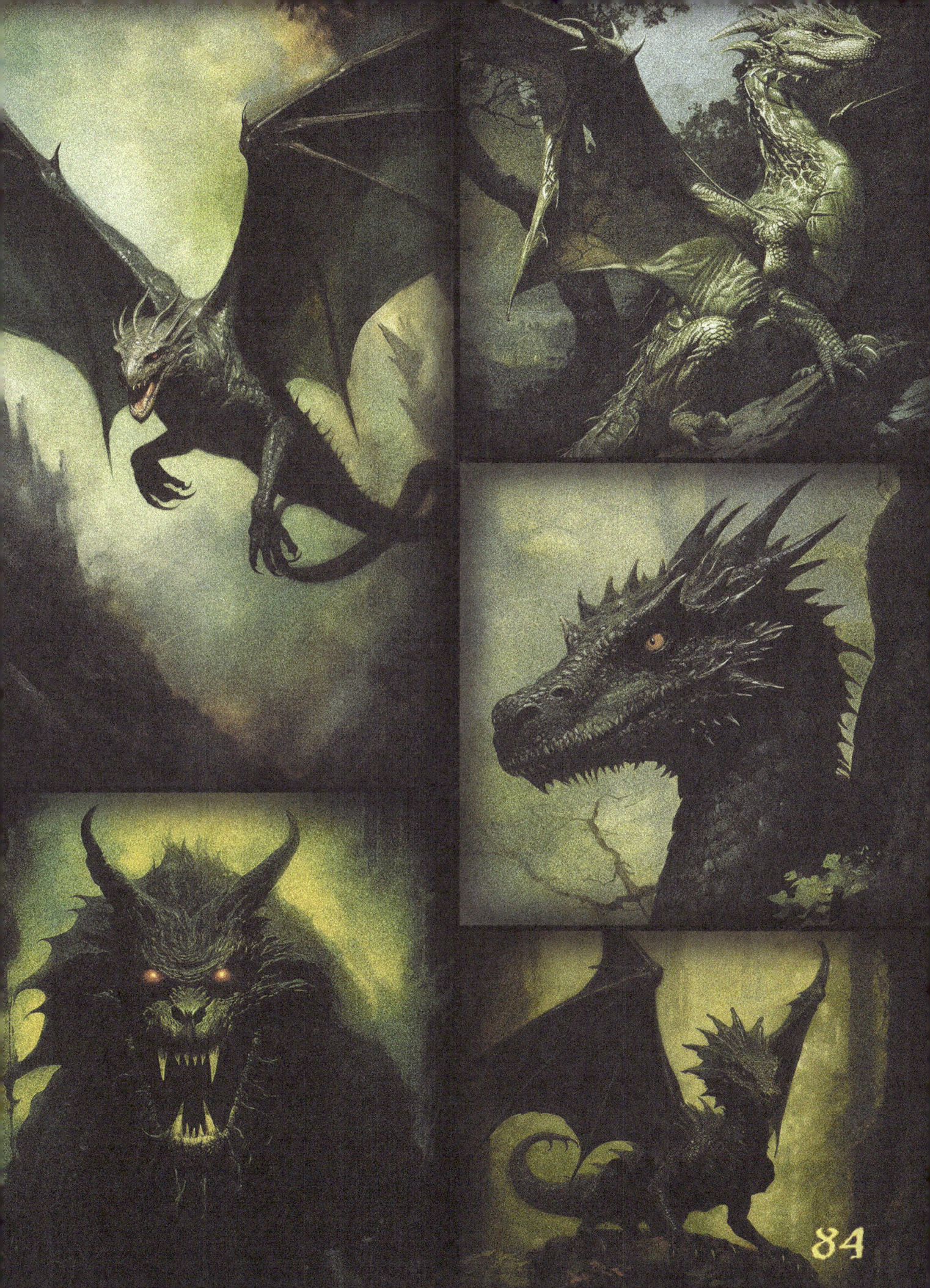

Gwyntorach dragons

Gwyntorach dragons have innate lightning abilities. Residing in the **Zephyric Regions**, but also at other high peaks across **Gwyn**.

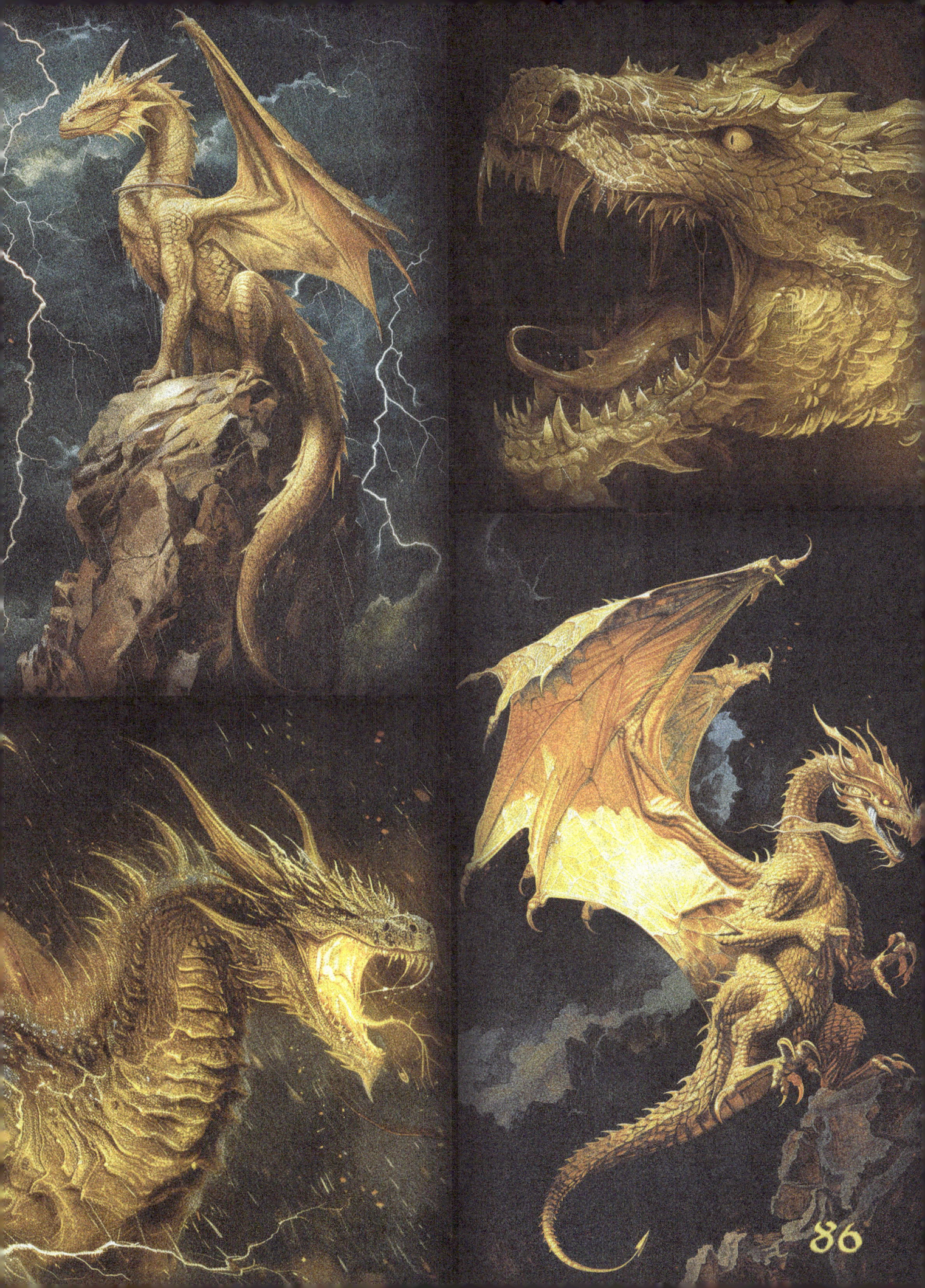

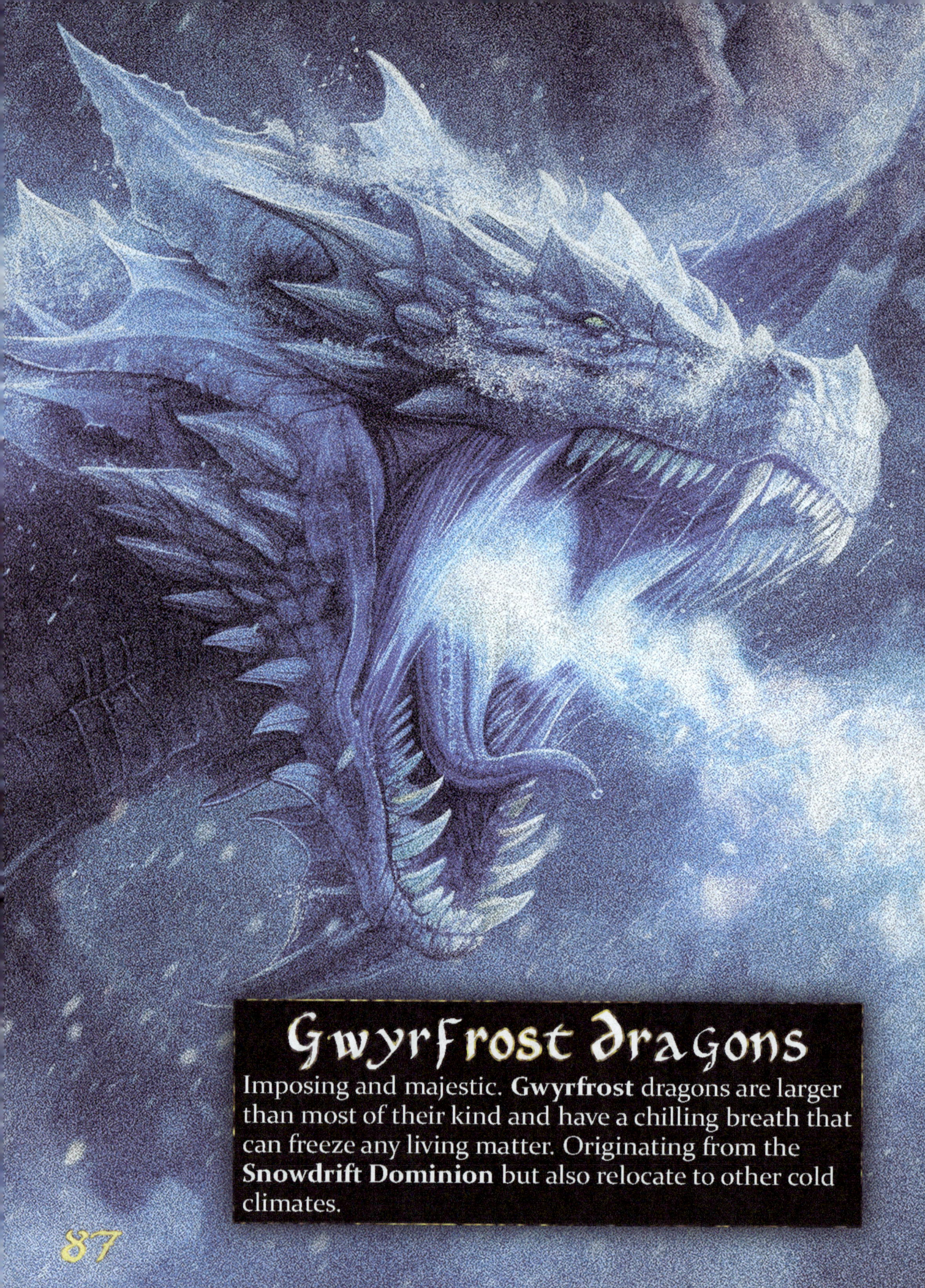

Gwyrfrost dragons

Imposing and majestic. **Gwyrfrost** dragons are larger than most of their kind and have a chilling breath that can freeze any living matter. Originating from the **Snowdrift Dominion** but also relocate to other cold climates.

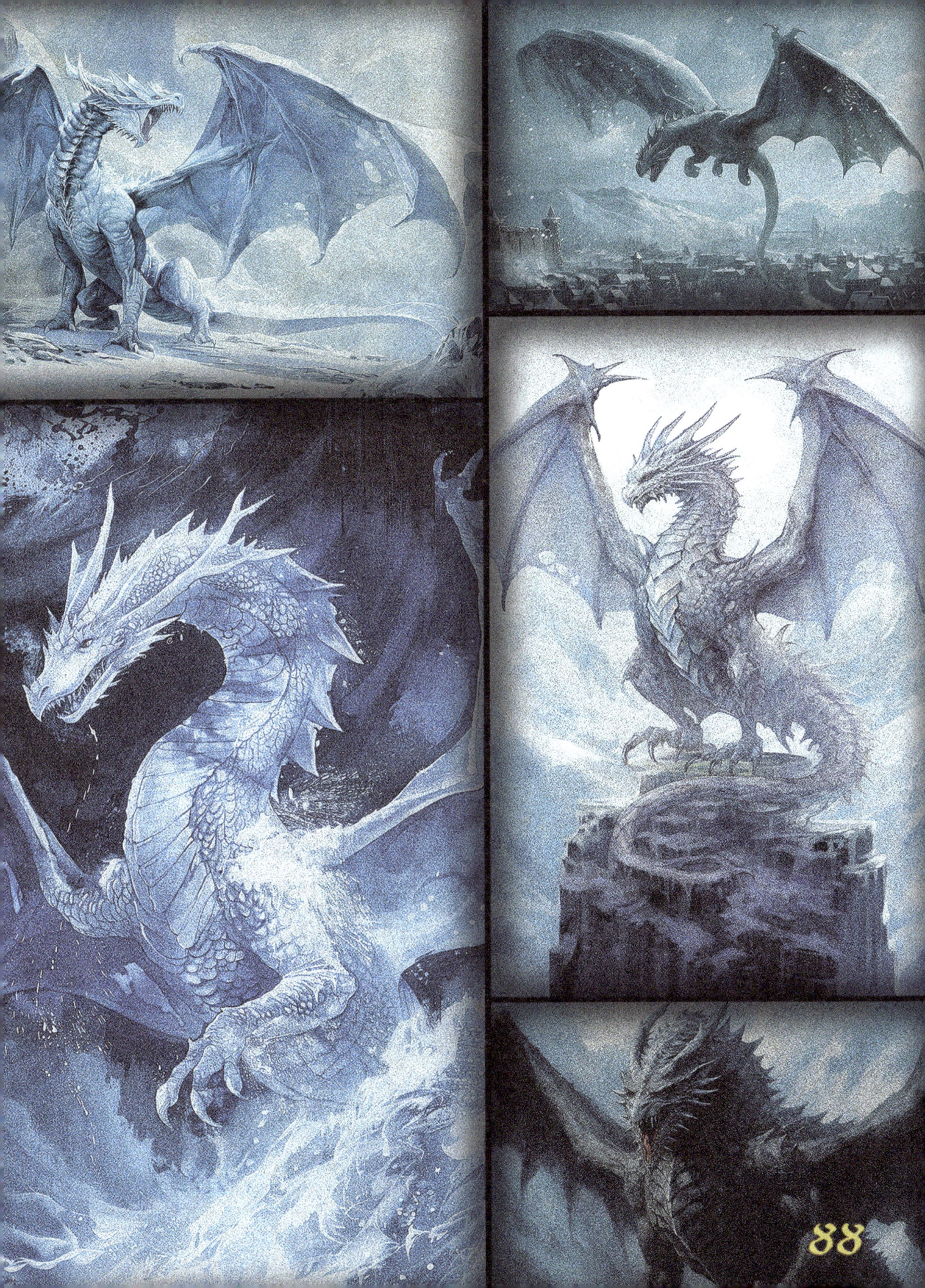

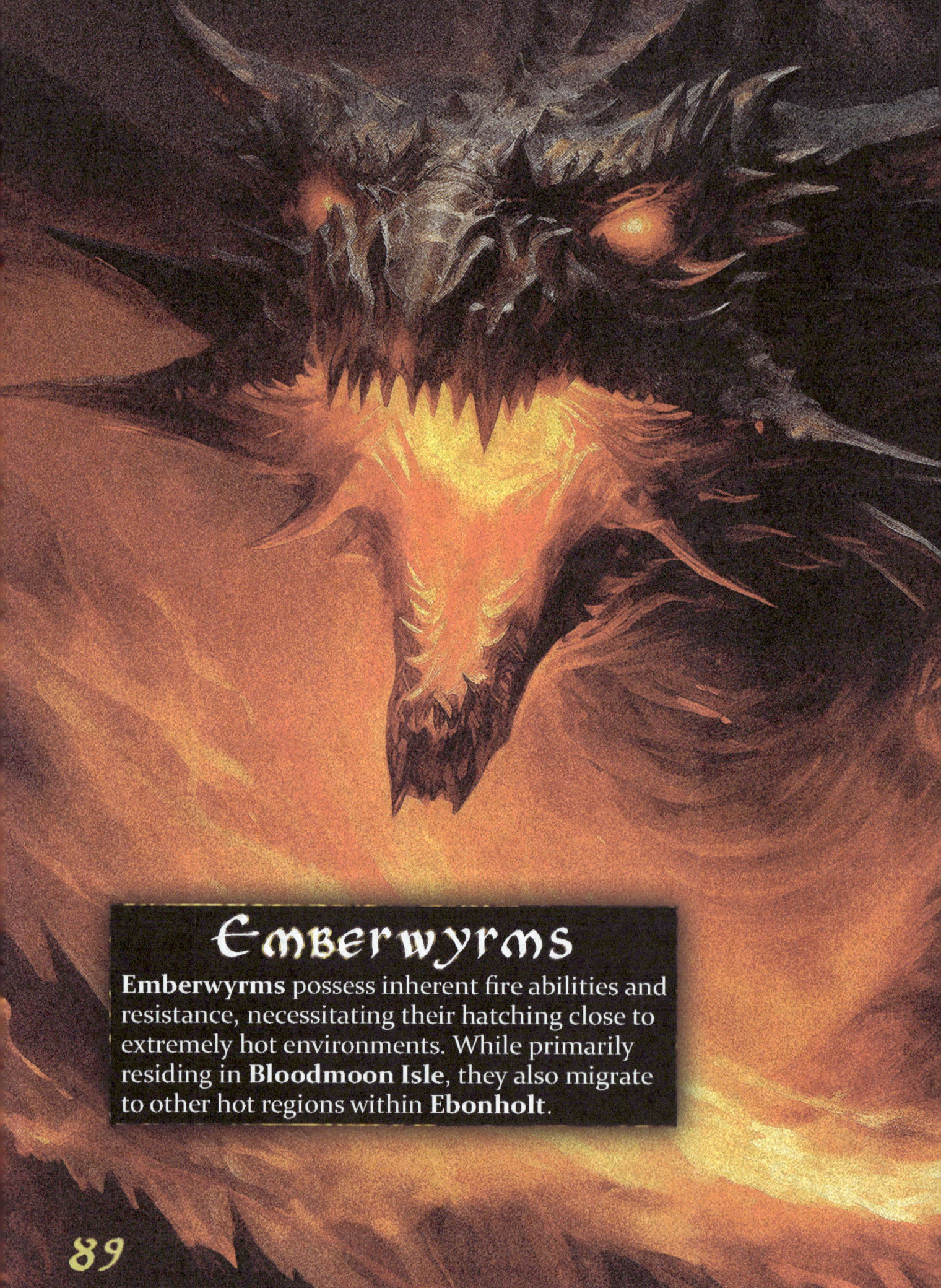

Emberwyrms

Emberwyrms possess inherent fire abilities and resistance, necessitating their hatching close to extremely hot environments. While primarily residing in **Bloodmoon Isle**, they also migrate to other hot regions within **Ebonholt**.

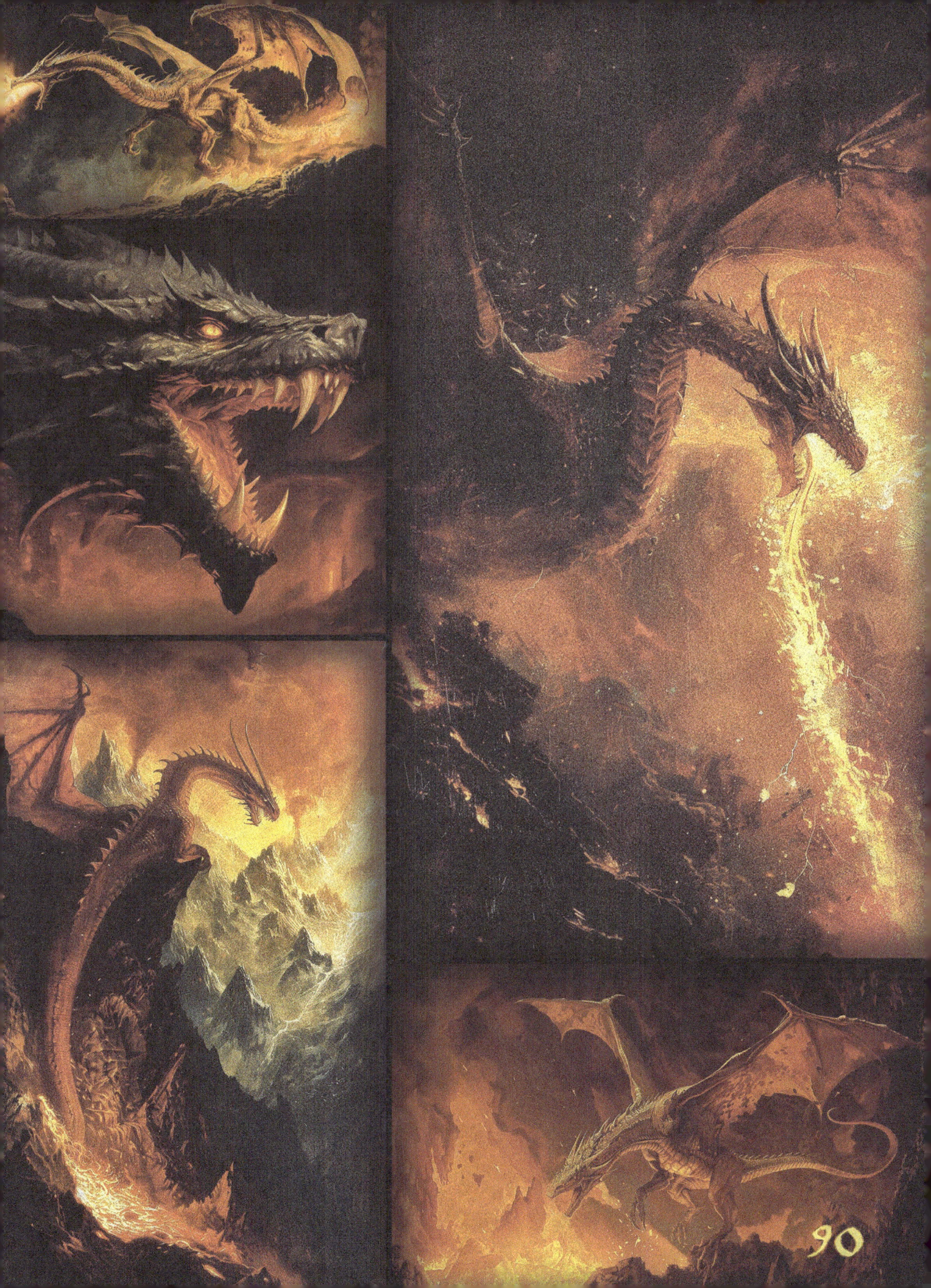

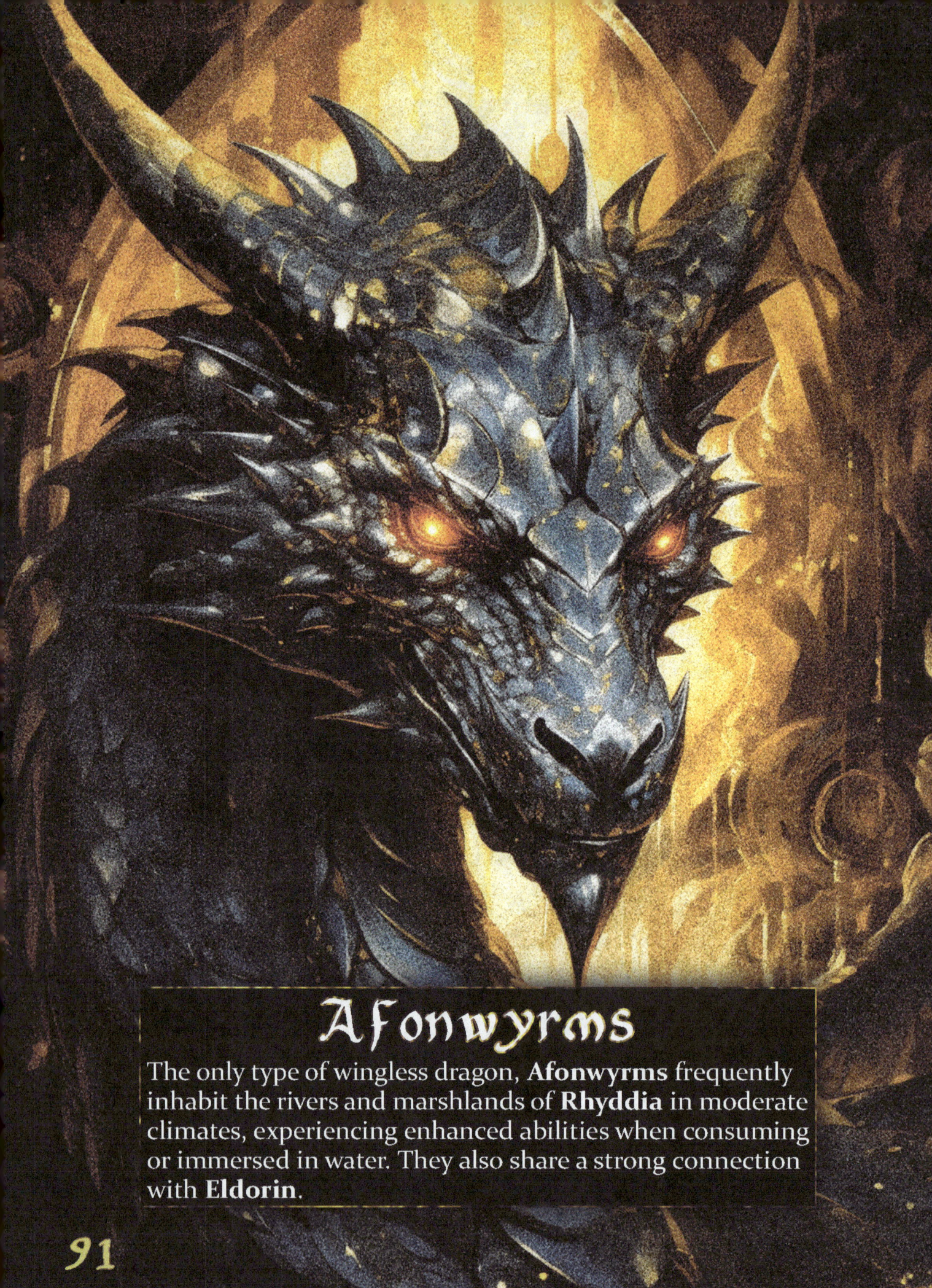

Afonwyrms

The only type of wingless dragon, **Afonwyrms** frequently inhabit the rivers and marshlands of **Rhyddia** in moderate climates, experiencing enhanced abilities when consuming or immersed in water. They also share a strong connection with **Eldorin**.

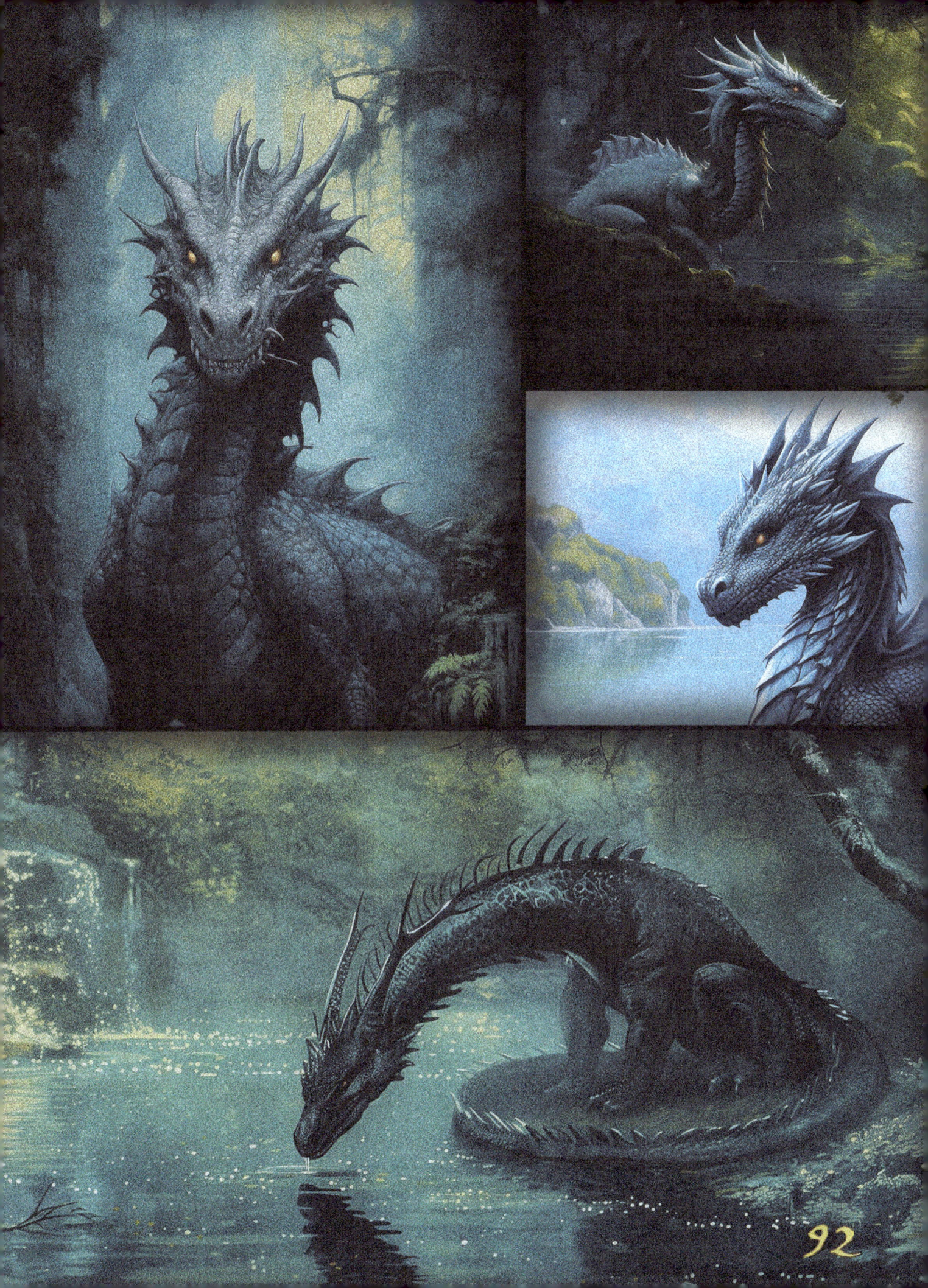

Morgalith dragons

Morgalith dragons are associated with the underworld, evoking fear and foreboding in those they encounter. They are the largest and most physically formidable dragons, originating from **Bloodmoon Isle**.

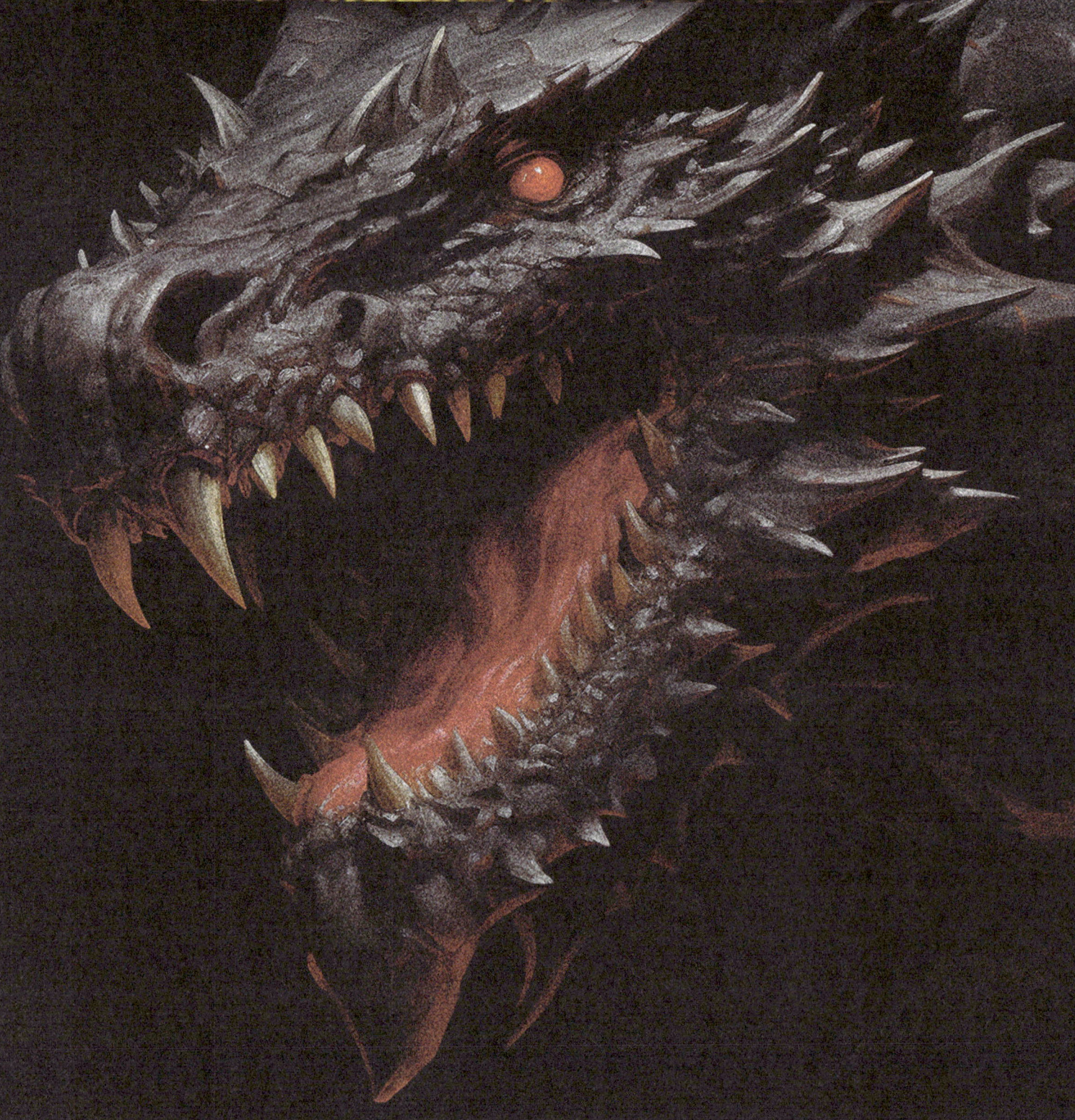

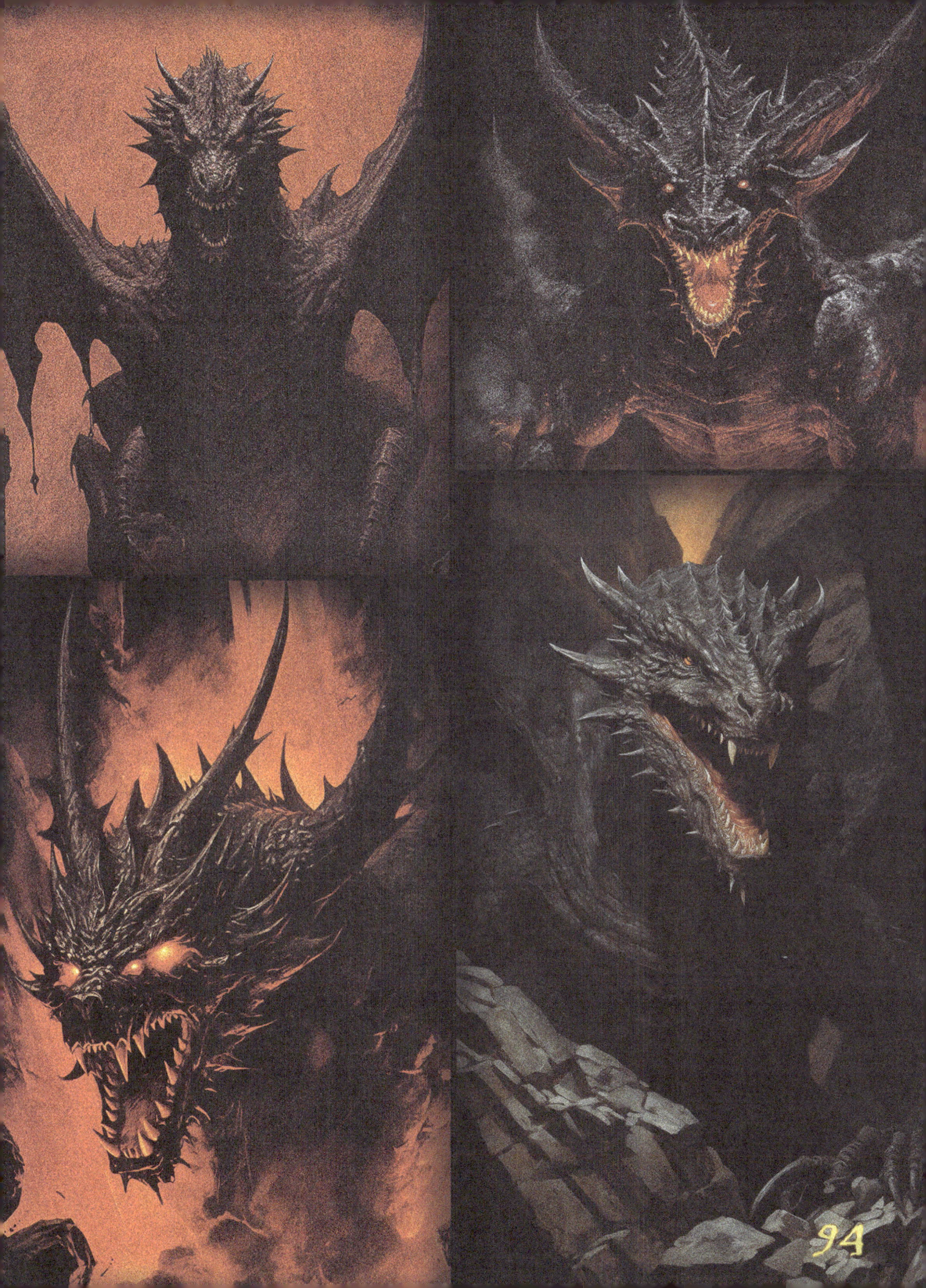

Dragon Riders

Dragons possess the ability to establish intelligent connections with individuals they consider worthy of sharing the skies with, entirely on their own terms. This occurrence is rare, with some suggesting that the dragon selects its rider based on their innate affinity towards the essence of the gods.

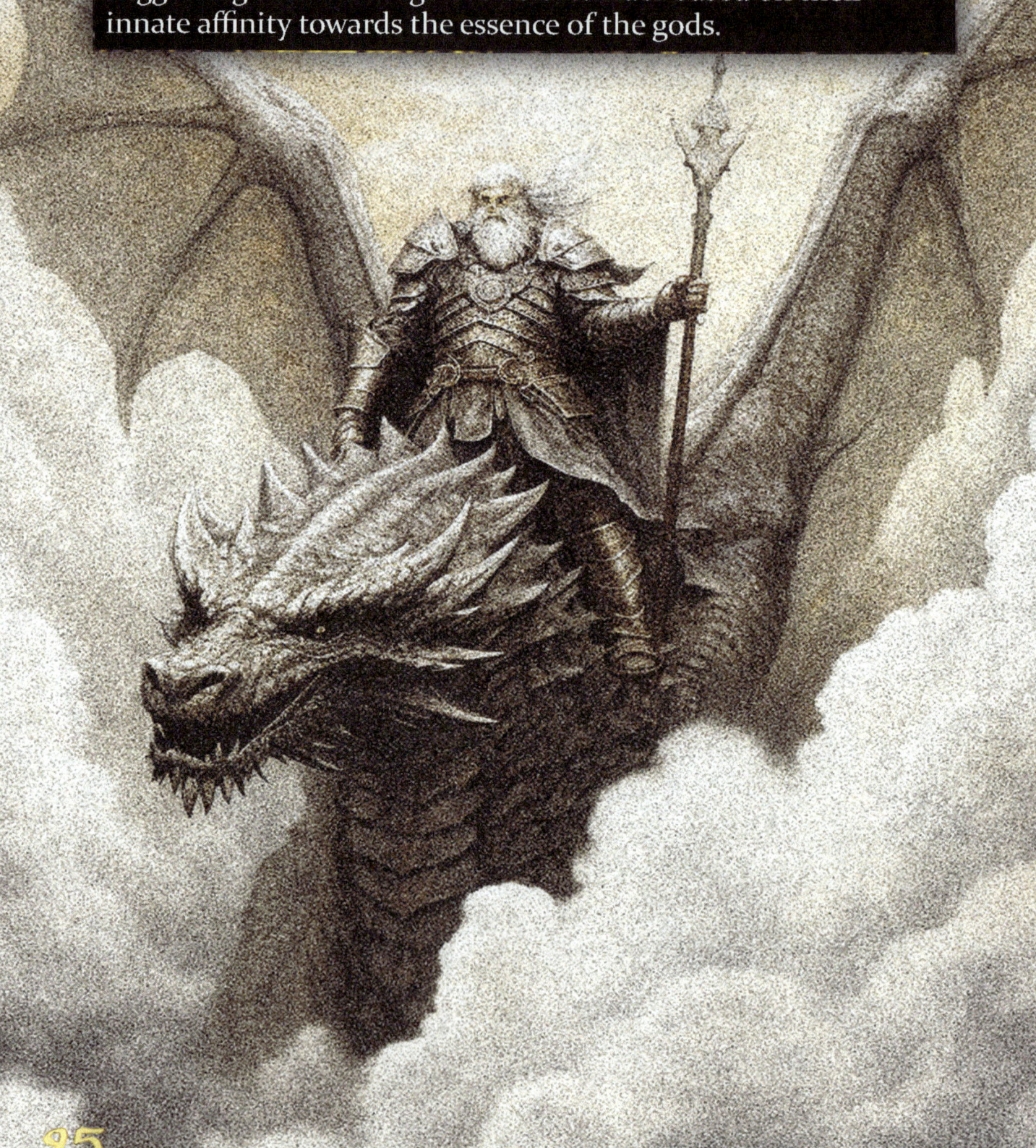

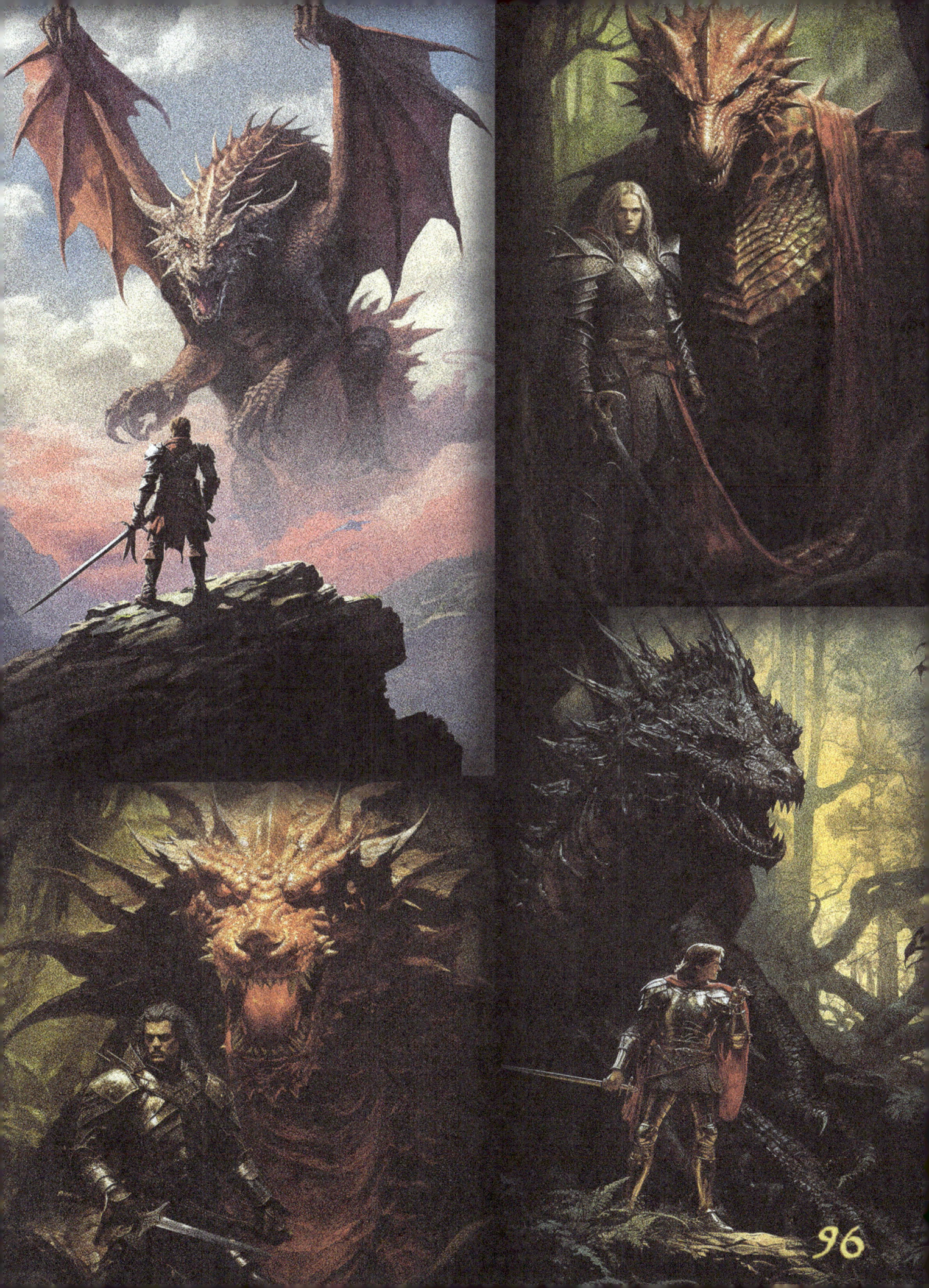

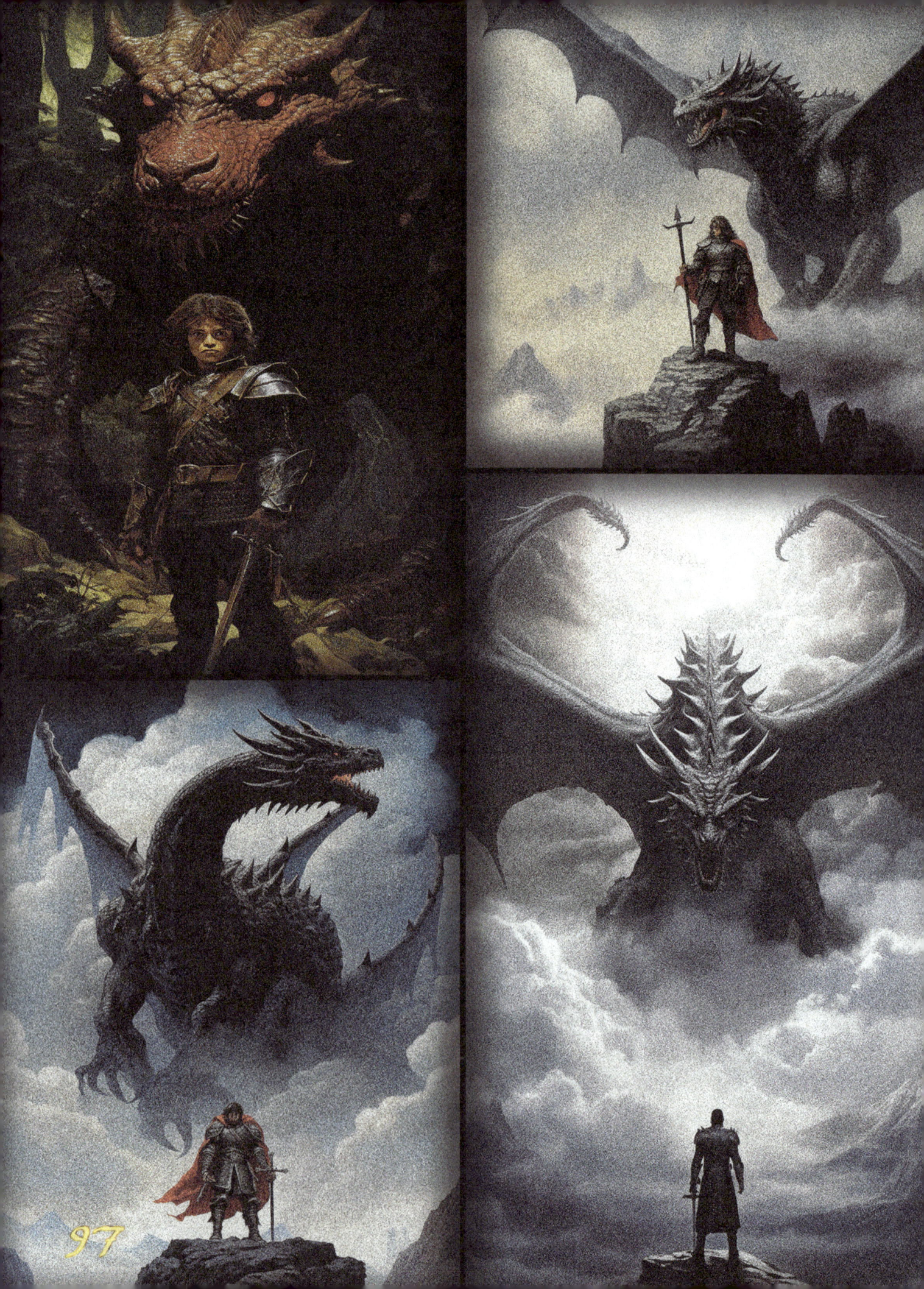

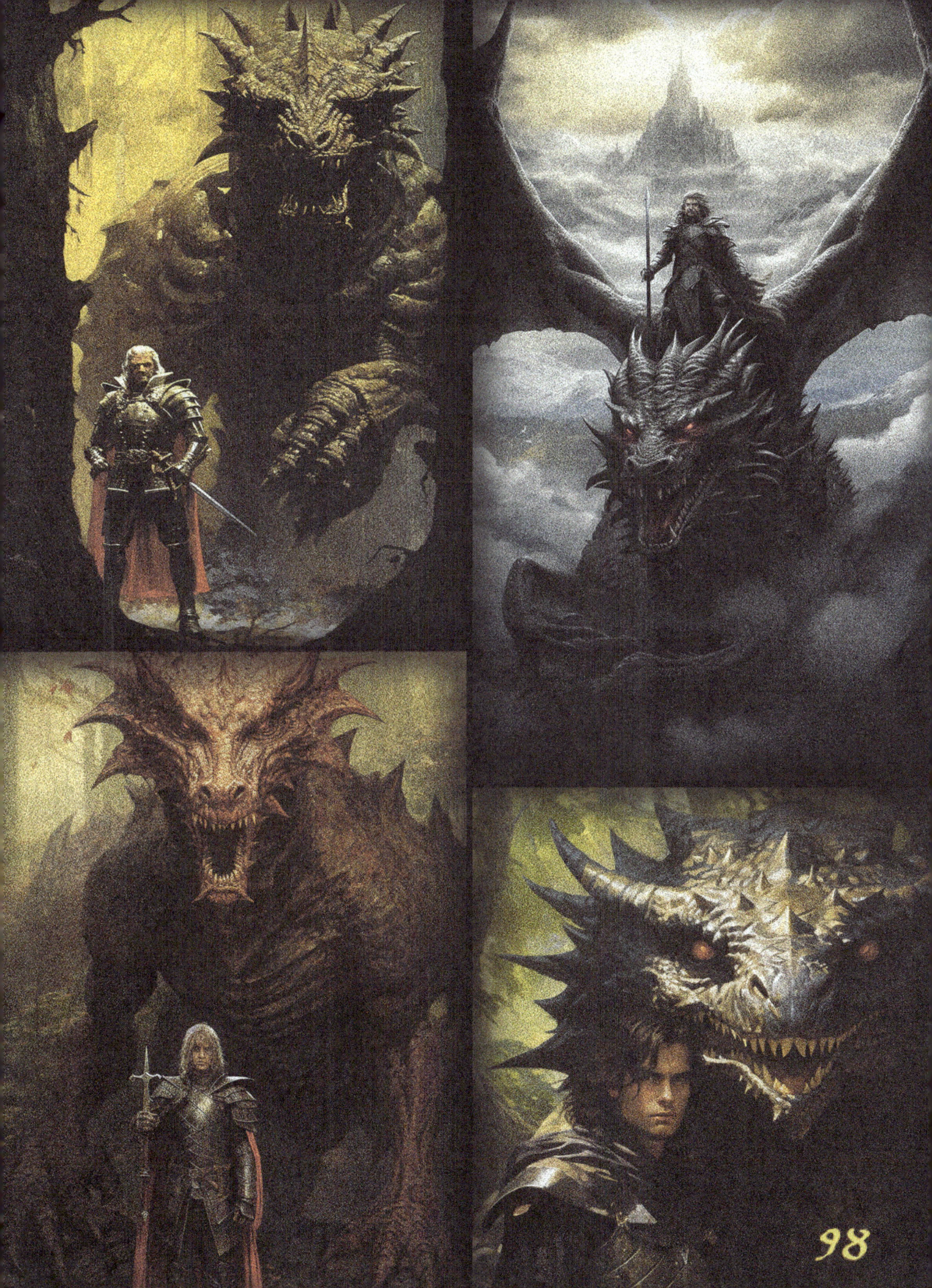

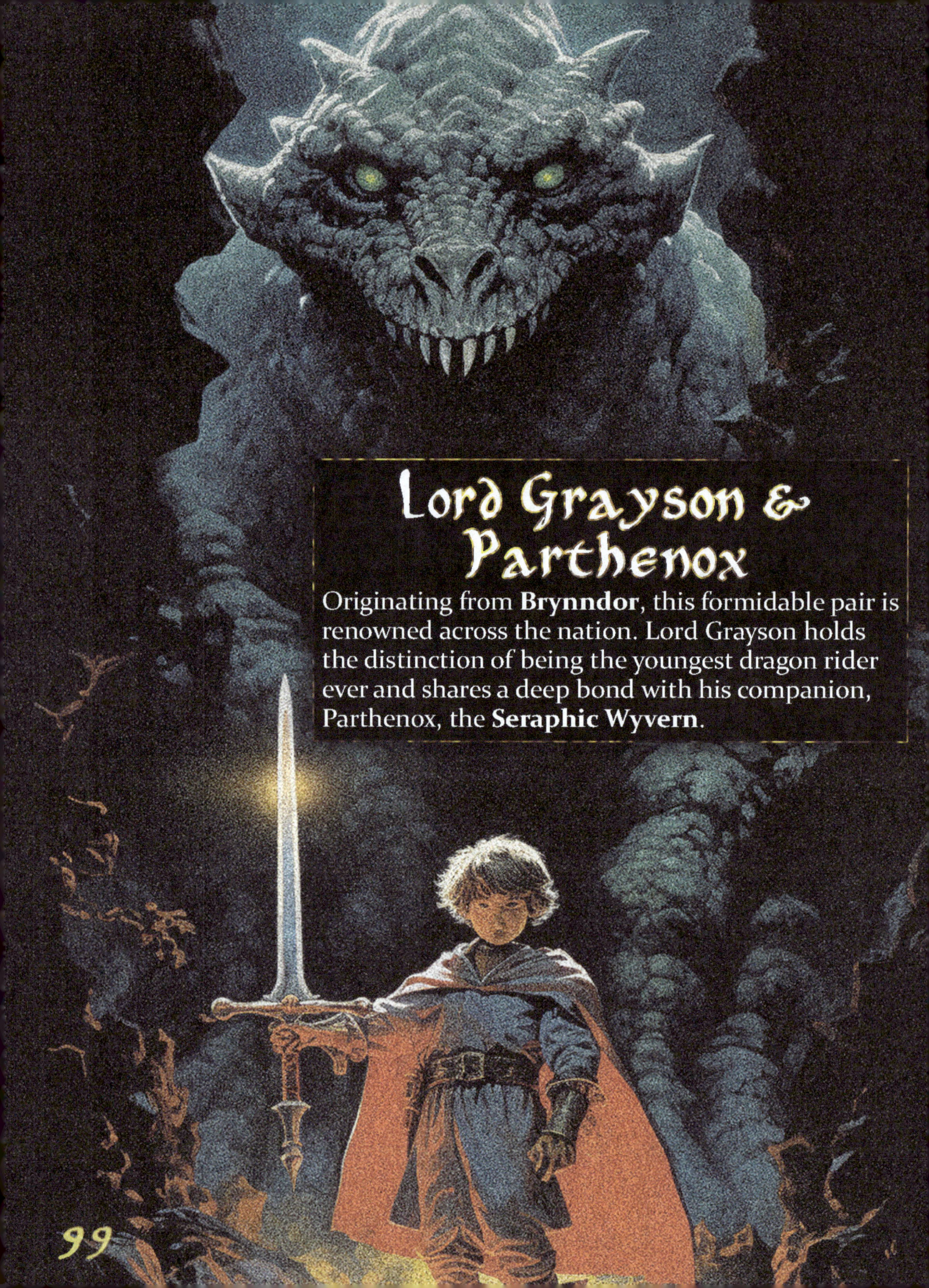

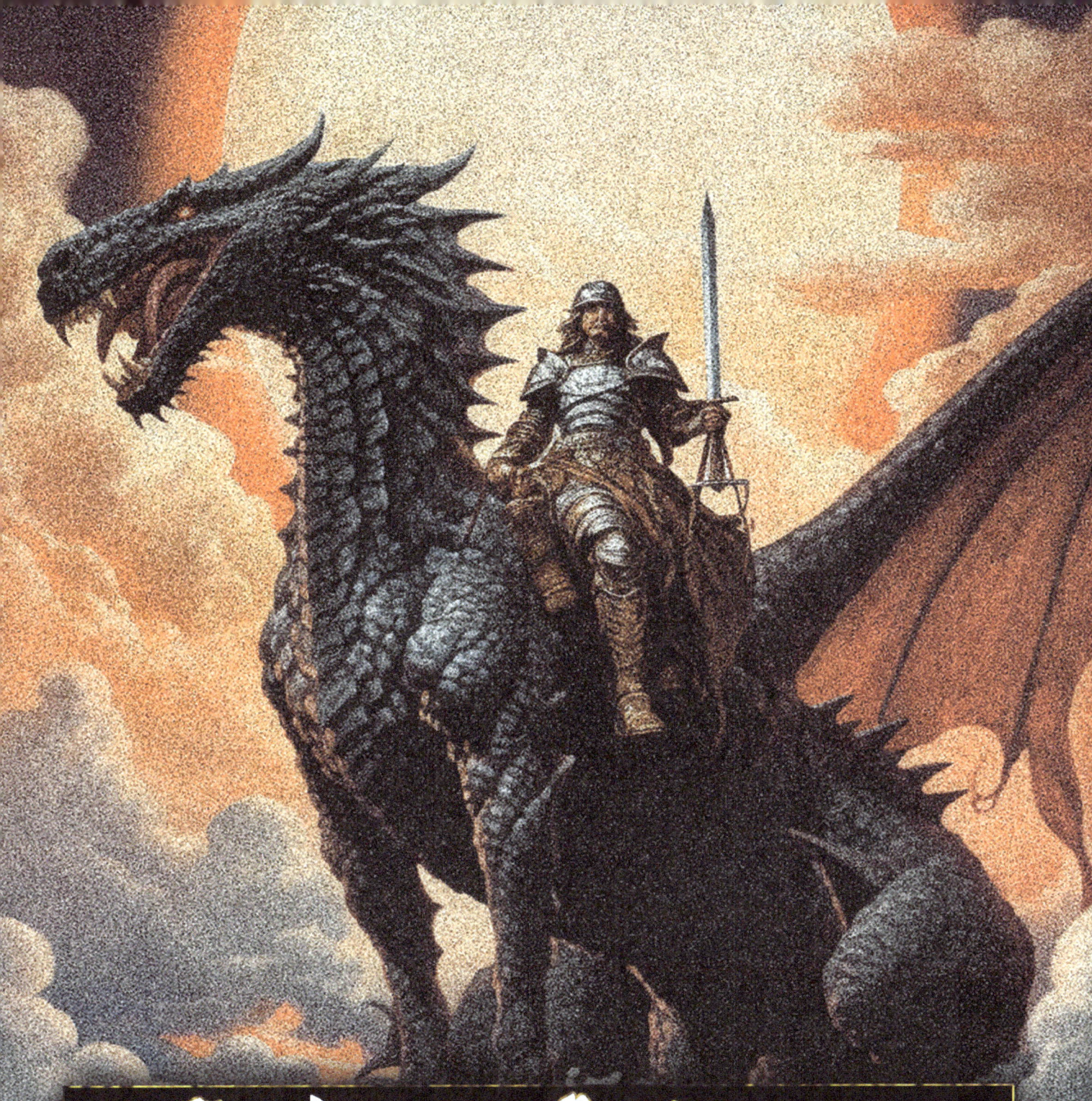

Sir Jeremy Bordeau & Axon Black Flame

One of the fourteen knighted by **King Morvus Blackthorn**, this duo commands respect. Sir Jeremy Bordeau is recognized for his strong relationship to **Ebonholt**, often journeying between there and other locations. He is partnered with Axon Black Flame, a smaller but fierce **Morgalith** dragon, known for the menacing black flames he exhales.

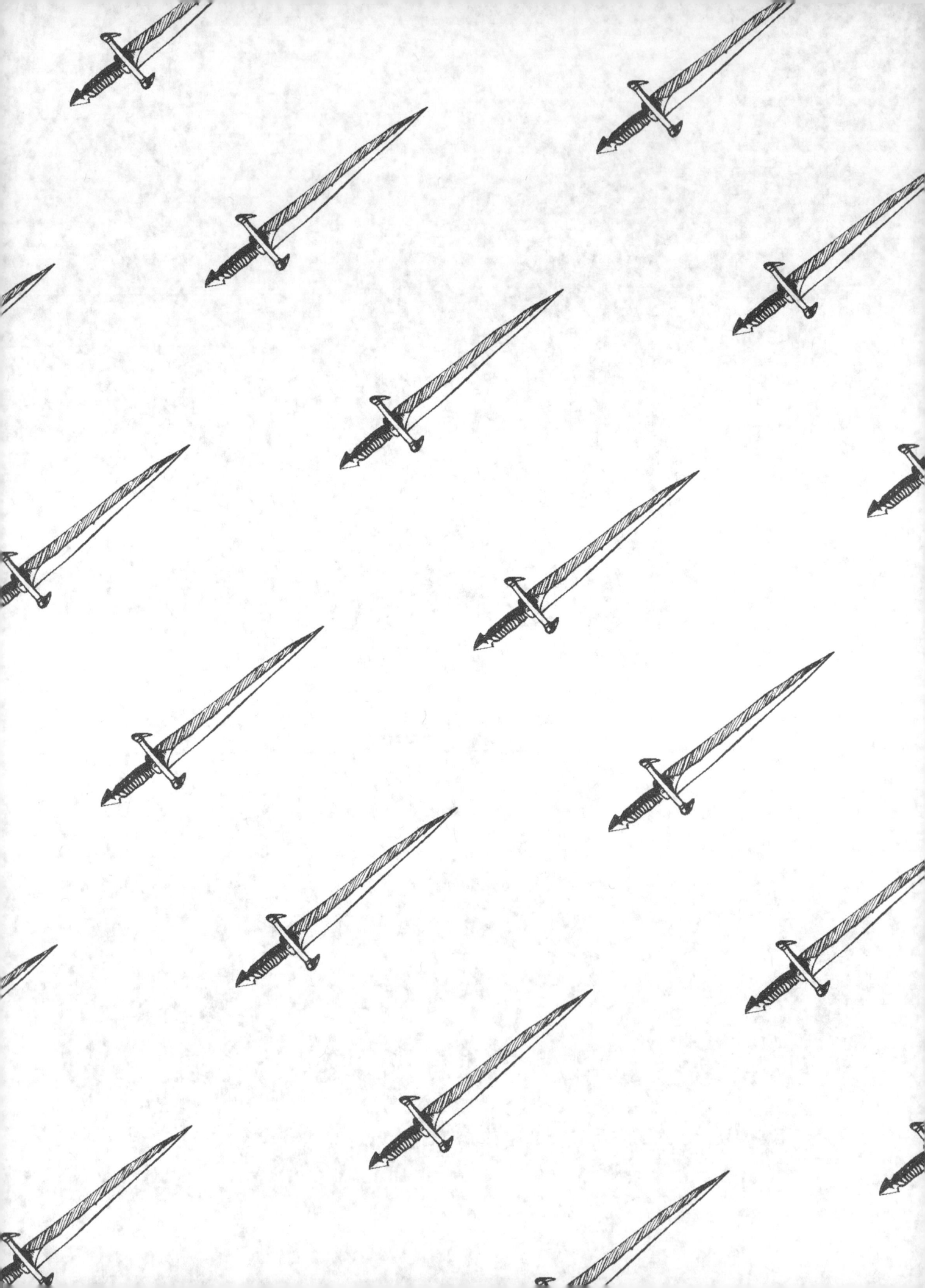